Lavochkin's Piston-Engined Fighters

Yefim Gordon

Original translation by Sergey and Dmitriy Komissarov

Midland Publishing

Lavochkin's Piston-Engined Fighters
© 2003 Yefim Gordon
ISBN 1 85780 151 2

Published by Midland Publishing
4 Watling Drive, Hinckley, LE10 3EY, England
Tel: 01455 254 490   Fax: 01455 254 495
E-mail: midlandbooks@compuserve.com

Midland Publishing is an imprint of
Ian Allan Publishing Ltd

Worldwide distribution (except North America):
Midland Counties Publications
4 Watling Drive, Hinckley, LE10 3EY, England
Telephone: 01455 254 450   Fax: 01455 233 737
E-mail: midlandbooks@compuserve.com
www.midlandcountiessuperstore.com

North American trade distribution:
Specialty Press Publishers & Wholesalers Inc.
39966 Grand Avenue, North Branch, MN 55056, USA
Tel: 651 277 1400   Fax: 651 277 1203
Toll free telephone: 800 895 4585
www.specialtypress.com

© 2003 Midland Publishing
Design concept and layout
by Polygon Press Ltd. (Moscow, Russia)
Line drawings by Aleksey Alyoshin and
Vladimir Tootikov
Colour drawings by Sergey Yershov

This book is illustrated with photos from
the archives of Yefim Gordon, Mikhail Maslov,
Sergey Komissarov, Helmut Walther, Keith Dexter,
the Central State Archive of the National Economy
and the Russian Aviation Research Trust

Printed in England by
Ian Allan Printing Ltd
Riverdene Business Park, Molesey Road,
Hersham, Surrey, KT12 4RG

Contents

Title page: A nice air-to-air of a late-production La-5F (Type 39) combining the all-round vision bubble canopy with the M-82F engine and small inlet.

Below: '14 White', another 'bubbletop' La-5F (Type 39), taxies out for a sortie.

Introduction

Birth of a design team

The design bureau led by Semyon Alekseyevich Lavochkin does not enjoy the same fame as other Soviet aircraft design bureaux – primarily because it was overshadowed in its main area of activity by the other Soviet 'fighter makers' after the Second World War, and most of its post-war designs were destined never to achieve production status. This book, however, describes the heyday of the Lavochkin OKB (*Opytno-konstrooktorskoye byuro* – experimental design bureau) – the wartime years; or, specifically, the aircraft which came into being during this arduous period. It was these aircraft which brought Lavochkin renown and played an important part in the victorious outcome of the Great Patriotic War of 1941-45.

The story of the OKB (and its first progeny, the fighter which would be known as the LaGG-3) began when Vladimir Petrovich Gorboonov, who headed the technical department of the People's Commissariat of Aircraft Industry (NKAP – *Narodnyy komissariaht aviatsionnoy promyshlennosti*) in 1939, had the idea of building a new fighter of all-wooden construction. He was, undoubtedly, guided by the assumption that the need for an urgent and drastic increase in the output of fighter aircraft would soon arise, and that aircraft production would be very probably hampered by the shortage of aluminium. Time soon showed that he was right on both counts.

The actual design work on the new fighter was largely performed by Semyon A. Lavochkin working under Gorboonov's direction. He had already gained considerable practical experience as a member of the design teams led by the Frenchman Paul Aimé Richard, Vladimir A. Chizhevskiy and Dmitriy Pavlovich Grigorovich.

During preparation of the early design studies Mikhail Ivanovich Goodkov, one more engineer from the same department of NKAP, joined the team; thus, a 'triumvirate' of designers came into existence. In the spring of 1939 this group submitted a report on their work to the then People's Commissar of Aircraft Industry Mikhail Kaganovich. The latter was quick in grasping the advantages of the design. Having obtained his approval, Gorboonov, Lavochkin and Goodkov were appointed heads of a newly established OKB in May 1939.

Above: Semyon Alekseyevich Lavochkin in front of one of the fighters he designed.

The first fighter designed by Semyon A. Lavochkin (together with S. N. Lyushin) was never built. It bears a close resemblance to the Grigorovich I-Z; note the recoilless guns developed by L. V. Koorchevskiy.

Vladimir Petrovich Gorboonov (left) and Mikhail Ivanovich Goodkov (right), the co-designers of the I-301 fighter. Both went on to pursue their own designer careers after completion of the LaGG-3 programme.

Above: One of the designs the future LaGG-3 was pitted against in the contest for the Soviet Air Force's new fighter – the Mikoyan/Gurevich I-201, the first prototype of the I-200 (aka MiG-1).

One more competitor – the Yakovlev I-26-2 (the second prototype of the future Yak-1), seen here during trials at NII VVS. The aircraft is cherry-red overall, with Yakovlev's trademark red/white striped rudder.

It should be noted that in 1939 the Soviet People's Commissariat (that is Ministry) of Defence called a contest for the development of a new fighter for the Red Army Air Force. In addition to the Lavochkin/Gorboonov/Good-kov team which offered the I-301, four other bureaux headed by Artyom Ivanovich Mikoyan and Mikhail Iosifovich Gurevich (the OKB of plant No. 1, later OKB-155), Aleksandr Sergeyevich Yakovlev (OKB-115), Vladimir Petrovich Yatsenko and Mikhail Mikhaïlovich Pashinin (OKB-21) submitted their designs – the I-200, I-26, I-28 and I-21 respectively. The outcome was strange, to say the least – three out of five designs participating in the fly-off (the I-301, I-200 and I-26) were cleared for series production!

The basic novel feature of the new fighter was the use in its construction of a material hitherto not used in the Soviet Union. It was the **del'ta-drevesina** ('delta-timber') composite, or wood impregnated with phenol formaldehyde resin (similar to the wood plastic which had been studied by Soviet engineers in the process of examining German wooden propellers).

At that time Leontiy Iovich Ryzhkov, chief engineer of a factory in Kuntsevo (then a western suburb of Moscow, now long since absorbed by the city) manufacturing propellers and aircraft skis had been developing methods of del'ta-drevesina production based on impregnating birch veneer with resin glue. The co-designers of the fighter project proposed that del'ta-drevesina be used in load-bearing structural elements such as wing spar flanges and fuselage longerons, where the use of this material offered certain advantages over ordinary wood.

L. I. Ryzhkov and the three heads of the fighter design team had some interests in common, so it was not surprising that the factory in Kuntsevo became the first production facility of the new design bureau. The team had to tackle a host of problems; the arduous work involved in resolving them helped form the core of the OKB's staff. It consisted mainly of former employees of A. V. Sil'vanskiy's OKB liquidated after the failure of the I-220 fighter. It was on the premises of this defunct OKB that the Lavochkin/Gorboonov/Good-kov team took up residence.

Acknowledgements

The author wishes to express his sincere thanks to Helmut F. Walther and Keith Dexter for supplying colour photos of Lavochkin aircraft preserved in Chinese museums; to Mikhail Maslov for supplying rare archive photos used in this book; and, as usual, Nigel A. Eastaway of the Russian Aviation Research Trust without whose assistance the book would have been so much the poorer.

Chapter 1

Birth of the LaGG-3

Wooden Wonder à *la Russe*

I-301 fighter prototype

Eventually the advanced development project (ADP) was completed and generally approved. In late June 1939 the Soviet Government issued a directive stipulating that two prototypes of the new fighter be urgently manufactured. As the factory in Kuntsevo proved totally unsuitable for aircraft construction, the new OKB moved to Plant No. 301 (hence the Lavochkin design bureau was later known as OKB-301 for security reasons). The new location had not been originally intended for aircraft construction either, being a former furniture factory. By 1938 the factory had already been re-oriented and was gearing up for manufacturing different versions of Caudron aircraft under French licence. To adapt these aircraft to Russian production standards, a special OKB headed by A. Doobrovin was set up at the factory. When Vladimir Gorboonov, Semyon Lavochkin and Mikhail Goodkov came to Plant No. 301 in the summer of 1939, the licence production plans had been abandoned and A. Doobrovin had been transferred to aircraft factory No. 135 in Khar'kov; however, most of his OKB's staff remained in Moscow, joining the design effort to create the new fighter.

Above: The first prototype of the I-301 fighter – the future LaGG-3. It was painted cherry-red overall and devoid of all markings.

The Soviet Air Force Research Institute (NII VVS – *Naoochno-issledovatel'skiy institoot Voyenno-vozdooshnykh sil*) located at Schcholkovo airfield east of Moscow approved the final version of the ADP, referred to as 'project K', in January 1940. When prototype construction started, the new aircraft was referred to in documents as a 'high-speed cannon-armed fighter with a structure featuring compressed wood'. After the OKB settled down at Plant No. 301, the machine received the designation I-301, the 'I' prefix denoting *istrebitel'* – fighter, as was the accepted Soviet practice at the time. (No mention has been found in contemporary documents of the I-22 designation previously referred to in many publications, and it can be assumed that it never existed.)

Another view of the I-301 during manufacturer's flight tests. The sliding portion of the cockpit canopy has been removed to improve the pilot's view; note the one-piece exhaust pipes, the stalky tailwheel strut with a very small wheel and the high gloss surface finish (the aircraft was carefully polished to cut drag).

Above: The I-301 at the NII VVS airfield in Schcholkovo, as revealed by the characteristic hexagonal concrete slabs making up the parking ramp. Note that the mainwheel well doors were entirely attached to the main gear oleos, featuring hinged lower portions which closed the wheel wells completely.

In 1939 the OKB had 93 employees on its payroll, but it had not yet achieved good teamwork. The relationship between the three newly appointed leaders was not absolutely trouble-free, as they sometimes had conflicting views on design aspects. Therefore the leaders of NKAP decided to confer overall responsibility for the OKB on one of the designers. The choice fell on Lavochkin as the most knowledgeable of the three.

The I-301's design process was long and laborious. The then-experimental VIAM-B-3 adhesive produced an unpleasant surprise: it contained a lot of phenol which irritated the workers' skin. The All-Union Institute of Aviation Materials (VIAM – *Vsesoyooznyy institoot aviatsionnykh materiahlov*) conducted extensive and urgent work at Plant No. 301, and appropriate safety instructions for working with the adhesive were drawn up.

There were pleasant surprises, too. The new adhesive permitted the bonded surfaces to be not quite close-fitting and even tolerated gaps up to 3 mm (⅛ in) wide because it penetrated deep into pinewood; the strength of bonded joints remained sufficiently high in these cases.

In March 1940, approximately a year after the beginning of the work, the aircraft was ready. The I-301 fighter had a sleek, aerody-

Another view of the I-301 at NII VVS.

namically clean look. The machine received a coat of cherry-red paint and was highly polished.

The I-301 was a single-seat low-wing monoplane. The fuselage was of wooden semi-monocoque construction. The fuselage skin, as well as that of the wings and tail surfaces, was made by glueing layers of birch veneer and plywood. The phenol-impregnated wood (*del'ta-drevesina*) was mainly used for the wing spars and local reinforcement of the structure. The wings comprised a centre section attached to the fuselage and two detachable outer panels. Three self-sealing fuel tanks were housed between the spars of the centre section and the outer panels. Landing flaps and ailerons featuring metal frame with fabric skinning were attached beneath the rearmost part of the wing. The stabiliser consisted of two halves joined to the fuselage.

The armament of the I-301 comprised Yakov Taubin's 23-mm (.90 calibre) MP-6 cannon placed between the engine's cylinder banks to fire through the propeller hub (hence the MP designation standing for *motornaya pushka* – engine-mounted cannon) and two synchronised 12.7-mm (.50 calibre) UBS heavy machine-guns (*ooniversahl'nyy [poolemyot] Berezina, sinkhronizeerovannyy* – Berezin versatile machine-gun, synchronised). Later the machine's armament was supplemented by a pair of 7.62-mm (.30 calibre) ShKAS synchronised machine-guns (*[poolemyot] Shpitahl'novo i Komarnitskovo, aviatsionnyy, skorostrel'nyy* – Shpital'nyy/Komarnitskiy fast-firing aircraft machine-gun) placed above the engine.

To achieve successful completion of the work, one always needs at least a bit of luck. For OKB-301 the appointment of A. Nikashin as project test pilot/engineer responsible for the manufacturer's flight tests was undoubtedly a stroke of good fortune. Speaking in advance of events to come, we may say that Nikashin performed his duties admirably.

On 30th March 1940 the I-301 fighter made its maiden flight. After performing several more flights Nikashin assessed the fighter's behaviour as satisfactory and the handling as simple; the aircraft could be mastered by pilots of average and less-than-average skill. On 1st May 1940 the I-301 took part in a flypast over the Red Square in Moscow along with other new Soviet aircraft.

The tests proceeded at a quick pace and were completed on 12th June. Two days later the machine was submitted for State acceptance trials. M. Tarakanovskiy was appointed leading engineer in charge of the tests, Pyotr M. Stefanovskiy and Stepan M. Sooproon were appointed as test pilots. The tests revealed that, with an all-up weight (AUW) of 2,968 kg (6,543 lb) the fighter attained a speed of 515 km/h (320 mph) at sea level and

Above: The I-301's instrument panel.

Above and below: The I-301 after a landing mishap on 11th August 1940 when test pilot A. Nikashin was dazzled by the setting sun on final approach.

Above: The wrecked first prototype I-301 after the engine cowling and the spinner tip have been removed, showing the metal propeller bent by the impact. The aircraft was repaired that time – only to be damaged beyond repair in a forced landing on 4th January 1940 after an engine failure.

A very early-production (apparently Leningrad-built) LaGG-3 in typical camouflage, probably during pre-delivery flight tests; note the small tailwheel.

Above: Apparently the first LaGG-3 manufactured by the Gor'kiy aircraft factory No. 21. Note that a landing light has been incorporated into the port wing leading edge and the hinged portions of the mainwheel well doors have been deleted. The extended flaps and colouring of the cowling panels are also noteworthy.

This still-unpainted Gor'kiy-built LaGG-3 overran after an aborted take-off at the factory's Sormovo airfield on 16th May 1941, collapsing the landing gear. The cause of the accident: a mechanic forgot to remove the clamps from the rudder and elevators! The poor chap was almost certainly jailed for this!

Above: This LaGG-3 (c/n 31213109) manufactured by plant No. 21 on 16th June 1941 crash-landed after a pre-delivery test flight and appears to be a write-off.

585 km/h (363 mph) at the altitude of 4,700 m (15,420 ft), and it took the fighter 5.85 min to reach the altitude of 5,000 m (16,404 ft).

Project engineer Tarakanovskiy called attention to the fact that the rated altitude performance of the I-301's engine proved to be 100 m (330 ft) less than that of the I-26 – a fighter prototype that had just been tested by the Yakovlev OKB (the prototype of the Yak-1). It turned out that the area of the I-301's carburettor air intake was insufficient. Besides alterations to the carburettor air scoop,

changes were made to the exhaust stubs, the wing flaps were fixed in the retracted position (for one flight) and the radiator flaps were fully closed. As a result, a speed of 605 km/h (375 mph) was attained at the altitude of 4,950 m (16,240 ft). Thus the I-301 fighter could be considered the speediest among Soviet aircraft powered by the Klimov M-105 engine.

The tests of the I-301 prototype lasted only for ten days during which 42 flights were made. Many faults and defects were rectified, but many things remained undone for lack of

time. For instance, the defects of the armament still had to be dealt with.

A decision was taken to continue the work on improving and developing the I-301, concurrently manufacturing a small batch of 25 to 30 aircraft of this type for service trials. A document assessing the results of the prototype's trials stated: *'In the I-301 aircraft the designers have basically tackled the task of creating an all-wooden aircraft employing increased-strength wood. It is necessary to ask People's Commissar of Aircraft Industry Aleksey I. Shakhoorin that NKAP pay greater attention to the development, testing and construction of the I-301 aircraft'.*

While the new fighter was undoubtedly of interest for the Red Army Air Force, 115 faults and defects were noted (apart from those of the armament); of these, 14 were rectified during the trials. The faults noted included, in particular, excessive heat in the cabin and excessive stick forces from the ailerons and elevator.

Development work on the I-301 continued. On 11th August 1940 a landing accident occurred when Nikashin was dazzled by the setting sun on final approach; the machine was seriously damaged, collapsing the landing gear. It was decided, besides repairing the first prototype, to speed up construction of the second example of the fighter. On 2nd October 1940, when both machines were due for rollout, a Government directive was issued

Another early-production LaGG-3, probably at the factory airfield. Note the original one-piece exhaust stacks, the unpainted heat-resistant plate just ahead of the windshield, the larger tailwheel and the straight rudder hinge line. The inscription in the top right-hand corner reads '1 Sekretno' ([Photo No.] 1, classified).

Above: LaGG-3 c/n 6271 undergoing static tests at the Central Aero- and Hydrodynamics Institute (TsAGI); the engine is replaced by a metal block of the same weight. The objects glued to the wing undersurface along the spars are designed to pop off as the wing bends, indicating critical stress levels.

Batch 35 LaGG-3s on the final assembly line at the Gor'kiy aircraft factory No. 21 (c/n 31213512 is nearest to the camera). The metal cowlings have yet to be painted. Note that the leading-edge slats were painted prior to installation, causing a disruption of the camouflage pattern.

Above: A nice shot of an early-production Gor'kiy-built LaGG-3 (c/n 3121715) during trials. Note the cannon firing through the propeller hub.

requiring all new fighter designs to have a range of 1,000 km (621 miles). The staff of OKB-301 were stunned by this directive. The redesign required to achieve this goal could set the development work several months back and put the machine hopelessly behind the competitors! Reworking the fuel system on an aircraft that had already been completed proved to be a major problem. But the design

team tackled this task admirably: two additional fuel tanks were to be incorporated into the outer wing torsion boxes.

But these measures were meant for production machines. They could not be implemented on the prototype because this would necessitate testing the reworked wing, and two precious months would be lost. Therefore an additional fuel tank of approximately 150

litres (33 Imp gal) capacity was placed behind the cockpit on the second I-301 prototype; the fuel from it was fed by gravity into the three main fuel tanks.

LaGG-3 production fighter
Subsequent events developed with extreme rapidity. The fighter's designers and test pilots were summoned to Gheorgiy M. Malenkov,

Another view of the same aircraft illustrating the clean lines of the LaGG-3.

a member of the Party's Central Committee, who immediately reported to Iosif V. Stalin about the main results of the work. A decision was taken immediately to put the I-301 into series production. At that time the Soviet Air Force changed its system of designations: all aircraft received new designations consisting of the first letters of the designer's name and a number (though the old system was used in parallel for development aircraft for a few more years). Accordingly, the I-301 received the designation LaGG-1. The improved version of the fighter with increased fuel capacity was designated LaGG-3. However, since all the plants involved began manufacturing the improved version right from the start, not a single production machine was completed to the LaGG-1 standard.

The designers' 'triumvirate' was drawing to a close. Semyon A. Lavochkin, together with most of the OKB's employees, was transferred to Plant No. 21 in Gor'kiy which became the chief plant for series production of the LaGG-3 fighter. Vladimir P. Gorboonov became Chief designer of Plant No. 31 in Tbilisi where production of the LaGG-3 was also planned. As for Mikhail I. Goodkov, he remained in Moscow and became Chief designer of OKB-301. As the first task he was entrusted with developing the installation of a 37-mm (1.45 calibre) cannon on the LaGG-3 fighter.

The decision to put the LaGG-3 into mass production meant that all work on the development and improvement of prototype machines had to be speeded up. Test-pilot A. Nikashin used the first prototype to check the machine's diving characteristics; then he began testing the armament and checking a new navigation instrument that had just been fitted to the aircraft – the direction finder. But on 4th January 1940 the engine's crankshaft bearings disintegrated in flight and Nikashin made an off-field forced landing, seriously damaging the aircraft. This time the first prototype was declared a write-off.

For a while, development work was continued on the second prototype; then it was decided that further work on it was pointless because the second prototype had single-spar wings, whereas the production machine featured two-spar wings, like the first I-301 prototype. A decision was taken to use production examples for further development of the LaGG-3.

The first production fighter was manufactured in Leningrad at Plant No. 23. To get series production going, a group of the OKB's employees was sent to Leningrad, and as early as December 1940 A. Nikashin took a production machine to the air.

When production machines built by Plant No. 23 went into service, reports began pouring in about engines prone to overheating,

Above: The upper part of the cowling hinged open for access to the dorsally mounted machine guns.

Above: The rear fuselage and tail unit of LaGG-3 c/n 3121715, showing the rudder mass balances and storage battery compartment hatch. Note the c/n stencilled on the fin and rudder above the star.

A cockpit shot of LaGG-3 c/n 3121715; some of the instruments appear to be missing.

Above: An early LaGG-3 with an engine-mounted machine-gun at a forward airfield during the Great Patriotic War. The aircraft has been modified locally by removing the lower portions of the main gear doors (to prevent fouling by mud and debris) and the sliding section of the canopy (to improve cockpit visibility).

An early-production LaGG-3 built by the Taganrog aircraft factory No. 31 after a forced landing in September 1941 with test pilot V. Antipov at the controls. Note the unusual design of the aerial mast. The purpose of the rope wound around the propeller spinner is unknown.

Above: A mechanic holds on to the wingtip as an early-model LaGG-3 taxies out from a snow-covered tactical airfield. The aircraft wears hastily applied winter camouflage which has already disappeared on much of the airframe. The small size and position of the star on the vertical tail is noteworthy.

Another LaGG-3 about to take off on a mission from a wintry airfield. This one still wears summer camouflage and a large tactical number instead of the star insignia on the fuselage.

Above: No, this is not mottled camouflage on the tail of this early LaGG-3 coded '22 Yellow' but just the shadow from camouflage netting under which the aircraft was hidden. This view shows well the design of the radio aerial.

A recovery crew takes a dismantled LaGG-3 away from the scene of a forced landing to the rear area on a GAZ-AA 1.5-ton lorry. This aircraft was adapted for winter operations, as indicated by the skid on the tailwheel strut.

Above: A late-production LaGG-3 coded '52 Red' in winter camouflage runs up its engine prior to a sortie. Note the more bulbous spinner and the rudder horn balance replacing the upper mass balance, both features characteristic of late production batches.

Above: '30 Red', a very exhaust-stained late-production LaGG-3, taxies out for take-off. Note that the rudder has been damaged and replaced and the missing portion of the red star not yet restored. The triple exhaust stacks characteristic of the late model are well visible here.

This LaGG-3 appears to be missing a good-sized chunk of the rudder – probably after being hit by German anti-aircraft fire.

Above: This early-production LaGG-3 is armed with eight launch rails for 82-mm RS-82 unguided rockets. It is seen here during trials at NII VVS.

Close-up of the RO-82 launch rails carrying RS-82 rocket projectiles with impact fuses. The RS-82 proved highly effective against ground targets.

An operational early-production LaGG-3 armed with RS-82 rockets taxies out on a forward airfield. This aircraft is fitted with six RO-82 launch rails augmented by bomb racks just outboard of the main gear units.

leaky radiators and hydraulics, and failures of push-pull rods in the control system. Gradually the defects were rectified and the new aircraft were issued to the regiments. The first regiment to receive Leningrad-built fighters was the 19th IAP (*istrebitel'nyy aviapolk* – fighter regiment) based at Gorelovo. It was followed by the 157th IAP which was part of Leningrad's air defence system.

Series production of the LaGG-3 in Leningrad did not last long. The precipitous advance of the German troops towards the city on the *Neva* River necessitated a speedy evacuation of the plant to Novosibirsk, where production of the LaGG-3 was not resumed. In all, Plant No. 23 built only 65 fighters, and the remaining uncompleted airframes were used for repairing LaGG fighters in the besieged Leningrad.

Before the war, production of the LaGG-3 (besides the already mentioned plants) was initiated in Novosibirsk, Tallinn and Dnepropetrovsk. Pre-war plans envisaged that 2,960 LaGGs (ie, twice as many as the envisaged number of Yakovlev fighters) would be manufactured by the end of 1941; more than half of this amount was to be built in Gor'kiy.

The arrival of Lavochkin and his team at Plant No. 21 in Gor'kiy was greeted without enthusiasm by their colleagues at the plant because they had hoped for the production of

the I-21 fighter designed by Mikhail M. Pashinin (Nikolay N. Polikarpov's deputy at this plant). Yet by the end of the first month Lavochkin's team succeeded in winning the confidence of the plant's personnel and imbuing them with enthusiasm for their fighter which by now was their common concern. This was due in no small degree to Semyon Lavochkin's personal merits. Being a person of high culture and exceptional self-control, he tackled the most acute situations with dignity and commanded great respect.

However, the objective difficulties associated with the introduction of a new aircraft type were great. The well-established production methods of the plant, which had previously produced Polikarpov I-16 fighters, had to be drastically changed.

The first Gor'kiy-built LaGG-3 took to the air on 23rd January 1941. After the first flight checks the initial production machine was transferred to NII VVS for the completion of the trials that were already behind schedule. From February to April the test personnel (the

This early-production LaGG-3 was captured by the advancing German troops in 1941. It is seen here before ferrying to Germany for evaluation (and accordingly a repaint in Luftwaffe markings).

already mentioned Tarakanovsky, Nikashin and armament engineer Berezin) determined the aircraft's behaviour in the dive and spin, characteristics of the armament and special equipment, studied the efficiency of the engine's cooling system. It was revealed that certain improvements in the handling could not compensate the weight increase of nearly 400 kg (881 lb). The engine cooling system became quite unsatisfactory; the engine was constantly running hot, rendering normal operation of the machine impossible.

Quite a few problems were associated with the fighter's armament. The MP-6 cannon developed under the guidance of Yakov Taubin and M. Baboorin and installed on the I-301 prototype was a successful and promising weapon. However, its recoil proved to be 2.5 times greater compared to what the armament specialists had guaranteed. Hence the cannon was replaced in the first batches by a 12.7-mm Berezin machine-gun.

Just before the war several LaGG-3 fighters were undergoing trials at NII VVS but these trials had to be suspended time and

Below: Another ski-equipped LaGG-3 (note the difference in spinner shape) during trials. The streamlined shape of the skis is noteworthy.

again because of serious defects. Only the first production machine piloted by Pyotr M. Stefanovskiy managed to remain airworthy to the end of the trials. As it turned out, the machines' maximum speed at 5,000m (16,400 ft) dropped to 575 km/h (357 mph), and it took the fighter 6.8 minutes to reach this altitude instead of 5.85 min. Even worse was the fact that the fighter was combat-capable only to a minor degree due to the aggravated temperature regimes of the engine and hydraulic system.

As noted above, neither the staff of the OKB nor the chief designer had any experience of building combat aircraft in series. Immediately after the launch of production of the LaGG-3 corrections to working drawings began to pour in. No fewer than 2,228 changes were introduced in February 1941 alone, most of them concerning design features. Complaints and demands (absolutely justified) were growing in number precipitously. Simultaneously, the new fighter with many bugs still to be ironed out was issued for conversion training to service units of the Air Force. In particular, the pilots of the 24th IAP at Liubertsy near Moscow started converting to the type.

A batch of aircraft that had been assembled and delivered to the regiment was found lying on the ground on their bellies the following morning – the undercarriages had collapsed. The defect could have entailed serious consequences if it had revealed itself during take-off or landing. It turned out that the hydraulic locks had become unserviceable during transportation. At Lavochkin's suggestion these units were redesigned.

A number of design flaws and production defects came to the fore during the first month of operation. For instance, a source of much concern was the spontaneous collapse of the tailwheel during the landing run which was accompanied by disintegration of the whole unit attaching the wheel strut to the fuselage frame.

In the course of one month 24 pilots were trained and converted in the 24th IAP. They were capable of taking off, landing, performing a 360° turn and the simplest aerobatic manoeuvres. The stage of more complex flying was not yet reached.

Another view of the same aircraft. The installation of skis gave the LaGG-3 a bigger ground angle because the mainwheel axles were located higher above the ground.

Opposite page, top: A fighter regiment lined up for some festive occasion, as indicated by the banner bearing the portrait of Vladimir I. Lenin, the founder of the Soviet state. The unit's ski-equipped LaGG-3s are lined up behind; surprisingly, very few aircraft wear the temporary winter camouflage

Opposite page, bottom: An operational (and very weathered) LaGG-3 carrying metal drop tanks on the bomb shackles.

This page: This LaGG-3 was used by NII VVS to investigate the type's diving and spinning characteristics in February-May1941. The photo on the right (taken on 6th May 1941) shows how a spin recovery parachute was installed under the rear fuselage on a tubular truss; note the actuating cable.

Above: In March 1943 LaGG-3 c/n 2745 manufactured by plant No. 31 in Tbilisi was used to verify various weight-saving measures aimed at improving the fighter's performance.

Above: Another Tbilisi-built example (c/n 6048) tested in March 1943. Note the angular windshield reminiscent of the Yak-1, a feature intended to minimise view distortions.

More plants join in

Many difficulties accompanied the launching of production of the LaGG-3 at Plant No. 31 in Taganrog under the supervision of Vladimir Gorboonov. Raw materials and equipment items were in short supply. Having delivered the first fighter in March, the plant succeeded in bringing up the tempo to one machine per day two months later.

The tempo was reached in May, and in August the Plant delivered as many as 130 combat machines. At that time Colonel Ye. Kondrat, chief inspector pilot of the Air Force for the North-Causasian direction, was tasked with setting up a fighter regiment equipped with Taganrog-built LaGGs for service trials and for the conversion of pilots who had previously flown other types of fighters. Kondrat was the first to shoot down a Junkers Ju 88 reconnaissance aircraft while flying an air defence mission in the sky of Rostov.

Chief designer of Plant No. 31 V. Gorboonov visited the regiment almost daily. He suggested that the pilots try out the first lightweight version of LaGG-3 developed by him. However, Gorboonov's experiment had a tragic end. Test pilot V. Goozin was unable to bail out when the aircraft's fuselage broke up during the transition from a dive to a climb, losing his life. Despite this crash, Gorboonov continued his attempts to retain this version of the LaGG-3 in production.

The launching of LaGG-3 production in Novosibirsk was lagging behind schedule. By the beginning of the war plant No. 153 named

Gor'kiy-built LaGG-3 c/n 312128100. Note the absence of the external radio aerial and associated masts; the aerial was housed inside the fuselage to reduce drag.

after Valeriy P. Chkalov had not built a single fighter. When the fighters finally began reaching front-line units, it turned out that their quality was the worst in comparison with the LaGG-3s manufactured by the other plants, which were already quite 'mature' by then.

Production machines had a poor surface finish, non-retractable tailwheel and external antenna mast. All this reduced the maximum speed by at least 50 km/h (31 mph) as compared to the I-301. The take-off run was no less than 500 m (1,640 ft) as compared to the prototype's 355 m (1,164 ft); rate of climb dropped by 50 per cent. One more problem surfaced – the aircraft suffered violent vibration at diving speeds in excess of 600 km/h (372 mph); hence a limit had to be imposed on the diving speed. A further unpleasant revelation was the defective bonding of stressed elements of the wing structure which afflicted production machines *en masse*; this necessitated a change in the production methods, and repairs had to be made to the machines already manufactured.

In his letter to Stalin dated 24th May 1941 Commander-in-Chief of the Air Force Lieutenant-General Pavel F. Zhigarev summarised the LaGG-3's service introduction period. He stated that, while the plans provided for delivery of 593 fighters and their issuance to fourteen regiments, in actual fact only 158 machines passed acceptance; of these, only 39 found their way to the regiments, the remaining machines being in need of refinements. Only 66 pilots had a chance to fly the LaGGs. The fighter posed no serious difficulties for service pilots converting to it who considered its handling to be easier than that of the MiG-3. However, persistent serious defects and incessant breakdowns forced Zhigarev to suggest that a number of regiments be equipped with MiG-3 fighters instead of the LaGGs.

Teething troubles

No other combat aircraft type was in such a pitiful situation as the LaGG-3 at the beginning of the war. Before July 1941 not a single regiment converting to the type was in a state of combat readiness. Initial service operation revealed a 'disease' manifesting itself in the fighter assuming high angles of attack of its own accord. As pilots described it, the fighter behaved like a spirited horse. All of a sudden, irrespective of the pilot's will, the machine sharply increased its angle of attack; the wing lift immediately decreased and the aircraft became unstable. As early as July 1941, four fatal crashes and seven non-fatal accidents resulting in the aircraft being written off occurred in service units of the Air Force involving the LaGG-3s.

The urgent intervention of specialists from the Flight Research Institute in Ramenskoye

Tbilisi-built LaGG-3 c/n 6011 at the factory airfield.

Yet another LaGG-3 built by plant No. 31 (c/n 6066). Like c/n 6048 on the opposite page, it has an angular windshield and fuselage-mounted gear doors enclosing the mainwheel wells completely.

Close-up of LaGG-3 c/n 6066, showing two 100-kg (220-lb) bombs suspended on the bomb shackles. Note the c/n painted on near the main gear pivots.

Above and below: LaGG-3 deliveries were hampered by accidents caused by production defects. This Novosibirsk-built example (c/n 0715373) suffered a mishap during a test flight on 1st April 1942.

(LII – *Lyotno-issledovatel'skiy instittoot*) made it possible to trace the cause and eradicate the defect. It turned out that a small counter-balance on one of the control system levers was quite sufficient to rid the aircraft of its dangerous habit. This new feature proposed by scientists found its way to the production line.

It took a fairly long time to eradicate the landing gear's tendency to collapse, mainly because it was impossible to eliminate leaks in the hydraulic system. Leaks of air in the pneumatic system used for cocking the guns made the LaGG-3's heavy armament unreliable. The first batches had three 12.7-mm Berezin UB heavy machine-guns (two of them synchronised) and two 7.62-mm ShKAS synchronised machine-guns. Starting with the fourth batch (July 1942), the heavy machine-gun between the cylinder banks was replaced by a 20-mm (.78 calibre) Shpital'nyy/Vladimirov ShVAK cannon, and the port side Berezin machine-gun was deleted. It was with this armament that most LaGG-3s were built in 1941.

Trials to which these fighters were subjected at NII VVS revealed that their performance had fallen drastically in the summer of 1941. Indeed, the rival I-200 (the prototype of the MiG-3) attained a maximum speed of 628 km/h (390 mph); the first production MiG-3 could reach 640 km/h (397 mph) and a typical production MiG-3 could do 615 km/h (382 mph). For the Yak-1 fighter these figures were 585.5 km/h (363.66 mph), 577 km/h (358.3 mph) and 560 km/h (347.8 mph) respectively. In the case of the LaGG-3 the I-301 prototype attained 605 km/h (375.77 mph), the first production example had a top speed of 575 km/h (357 mph) and mass production machines could only reach 549 km/h (341 mph). And consider that this performance was achieved with the radiator flap fully closed.

The same was true for rate of climb – another important parameter for a fighter. While the I-301 prototype needed 5.85 min to climb to 5,000 m, a production LaGG-3 required 8.6 minutes.

This was due in part to the fighter being too heavy for the M-105P engine which delivered 1,050 hp at 4,000 m (13,123 ft). Right from the first production batches attempts were made to bring down the fighter's weight. In particular, the fuel load was reduced from 410 kg (904 lb) to 340 kg (750 lb); the designers believed that a range of 705 km/437 miles at 0.9 of the maximum speed was quite suffi-

cient. The overall payload was reduced by more than 100 kg (220 lb). Still, deteriorating production standards caused the fighter to become steadily heavier, and, in consequence, the AUW was finally reduced by just 56 kg (123 lb).

Discouraging results were obtained when the LaGG-3 was tested for diving. At high speeds the sliding cockpit canopy frame became deformed and the landing gear doors sometimes tore away.

Speaking of the poor manufacturing standards of the LaGG-3 fighter, it is worth mentioning a document prepared by leading engineer M. Tarakanovskiy after the inspection of aircraft c/n 3121715 which had arrived at NII VVS. He found nine serious defects which had to be rectified before the fighter could be cleared for combat operation.

One can imagine the feelings of Semyon Lavochkin, at that time Chief designer of Plant 21 in Gor'kiy – the principal production plant, when he received complete information on the fighter. Complaints against the LaGG-3 were all the more unnerving because the situation with the other fighter that had been born almost at the same time – the Yak-1 – looked much better.

Lavochkin racked his brains in search of a solution. He understood that the war was devouring aircraft by the thousand. To avoid hampering their mass production, their design features had to remain stable. Lavochkin's difficult task was compounded by the fact that three more plants were totally dependent on the Gor'kiy plant and could not even eliminate defects without receiving drawings from it.

Variations on the armament theme

Various versions of armament were actively experimented with in the autumn of 1941. A small batch of LaGG-3s was completed with a 23-mm (.90 calibre) Volkov/Yartsev VYa-23 cannon between the cylinder banks of the M-105P engine. Lavochkin continued the work initiated by M. Goodkov, installing a 37-mm cannon designed by Boris Shpital'nyy or a different cannon of the same calibre designed by A. Nudel'man and A. Sooranov between the cylinder banks.

Lavochkin was the first among Soviet fighter designers to install direction finders on production machines. The first six LaGGs so equipped successfully passed service trials in the 24th IAP when repelling the enemy air raids against the capital. As for improving the radio equipment, this work did not proceed quite so effectively at that tome. All LaGGs had been fitted with at least a receiver, but the quality of radio communication was poor, reception being hampered by noise.

Gradually the configuration of the mass-production LaGG-3 was taking shape at the production line in Gor'kiy. Starting with the 11th batch (October 1941), the armament was reduced to one ShVAK cannon and one UBS machine-gun. Racks for six 82-mm (≈ 3¼ in) RS-82 rocket projectiles under the wings became a standard fit. The fuel load was reduced to 260 kg (573 lb); hence provision was made for using drop tanks in order to compensate for the shorter range on internal fuel. The designers succeeded in bringing the all-up weight down to 3,080 kg (6,790 lb), but attempts to further reduce it continued. In the autumn of 1941 the LaGG-3 occupied a notable place among front-line fighters. By the beginning of the 'decisive' German offensive against Moscow 170 LaGGs (that is, 18 per cent of the Red Army Air Force's total number of fighters) were operational, and by the beginning of the Soviet counter-offensive this number rose to 263 (26 per cent). This was due in part to the fact that the plant in Gor'kiy had not been forced to evacuate and the volume of production of the LaGGs – as the only ones among combat machines – suffered almost no curtailing in the late autumn of 1941. During November – the most difficult month – Lavochkin fighters made up more than half of the total output of combat machines. In all, by the end of 1941 a total of 1,659 LaGGs were built in Gor'kiy, 474 in Taganrog, 265 in Novosibirsk and 65 in Leningrad, amounting to a grand total of 2,463 aircraft, or 83 per cent of what had been planned before the war.

Ongoing production problems

Lavochkin's design team had high hopes for turning the Novosibirsk plant into a major centre for manufacturing LaGG-3 fighters. However, these hopes never came true – first and foremost because on 30th October 1941 Aleksandr S. Yakovlev arrived there together with his design team. This is how Yakovlev described the situation at the plant in his book *The Goal of Life*:

'For about a year the Siberian plant had been tasked with manufacturing LaGG-3 fighters, but work on this aircraft proved to be in a very pitiful state. By the time of our arrival the plant was crammed with unfinished aircraft. Not only the assembly shop but the other workshops were turned into a 'swamp', too. During the recent months no combat-ready machines had been delivered.'

Yakovlev came to the conclusion that the main reason for this deplorable state of affairs was the extremely poor technological preparation of production.

Indeed, line-flow production had not yet been introduced at the majority of aircraft plants at the time. Thus, in the final assembly shop all operations from the first one to the last one were effected at the same place by one or several teams of workers wandering

Above and below: This late-production ski-equipped LaGG-3 crashed on landing during trials (probably at an overhaul plant, since the aircraft is obviously far from new).

Maintenance work under way on a LaGG-3 in field conditions. This picture shows how the engine could be exposed almost completely.

This LaGG-3 was used to investigate the possibility of increasing the fighter's speed by means of VRD-1 ramjet boosters developed by M. Bondaryuk.

from one aircraft to another. The smallest delay or hitch at any of the assembly jigs seriously hampered or even stopped the process in the final count.

The situation was compounded by the harsh winter that had set in. Chaotically parked fighters disappeared under a metre-thick layer of snow. One could see tails, propeller spinners and aerial masts protruding from beneath the snow… Production teams had to organise veritable archeological excavations. All this took place at the time when the front needed as many combat aircraft as possible. Yakovlev writes further:

'Before the October holidays (the anniversary of the Bol'shevik revolution, actually on 7th November – translator's note) one of the leaders of the regional committee of the Communist Party arrived at the factory. A month earlier the plant's leadership had solemnly sworn to deliver 30 LaGG-3 aircraft by the anniversary of the Revolution, but in the situation that arose not a single aircraft could be delivered.'

Here Yakovlev's statement can be disputed. In October, having surmounted numerous difficulties, the plant built 63 LaGG-3 fighters, or three and a half as many as in the preceding month. They were supplemented by 54 LaGGs in November and 97 more in December. Director of Plant No. 153 Romanov and representative of the State Defence committee at the factory General Leshookov, who had reported that there were no obstacles for organising a normal tempo of deliveries and increasing the number of LaGG-3s produced, were accused of incompetence by Yakovlev. He repeatedly made telephone calls to Stalin and asked for the unwanted leaders to be removed from office.

Let us turn to Yakovlev's book again:

'In the first half of January 1942 we got another telephone call from Stalin. After enquiring about the progress of the work he informed us that the State Defence Committee had taken a decision to switch the Siberian plant completely to the manufacture of Yaks and transfer LaGG-3 production to another plant. The plant was instructed to halt all work on LaGGs immediately and to organise line-flow production of Yak-7 fighters.

"Yaks and LaGGs come close to each other in their performance, but pilots have a greater liking for Yaks", said he. "The Yaks have better manoeuvrability and are free from some defects revealed on the LaGG-3 at the frontlines. In the coming days you shall receive a document on this score, and now start the reorganisation of production immediately."'

Thus, using his political clout as Deputy People's Commissar of Aircraft Industry, Yakovlev succeeded in lobbying a decision on the final phasing out of Lavochkin's machine from production and promoting his own fighter. To secure his success, Yakovlev sent his 'emissaries' to Gor'kiy with a view to occupying the production line of plant No. 21 as well. This plant, one of the largest Soviet aircraft factories, was engaged in a massive effort aimed at improving the performance and combat capabilities of the LaGG-3 fighter. Tests conducted at the plant gave encouraging results: the fighter's speed increased to 490 km/h (304 mph) at sea level and 580 km/h (360 mph) at the second engine-rated altitude; the vertical manoeuvrability was also improved. However, these results were not corroborated by NII VVS which was a State controlling authority empowered to conduct tests.

A LaGG-3 from the 23rd production batch tested in March-April 1942 attained a maximum speed of only 446 km/h (277 mph) at sea level and 518 km/h (321 mph) at 5,100 m (16,732 ft). A climb to 5,000 m (16,404 ft) took

7.1 min. These figures were obtained at the all-up weight of 3,100 kg (6,843 lb) which included the weight of rocket projectiles together with attachments and guide rails. When the underwing racks were removed, the maximum speed rose by 20 km/h (12 mph). However, removal of the sliding cockpit canopy – a forced measure in order to improve visibility – and opening the radiator flap still further to avoid engine overheating (that was the way service pilots flew the LaGG-3 at that time) led to the conclusion that the LaGG-3's maximum speed was close to 500 km/h (310 mph).

Complaints were made concerning the fighter's poor manoeuvrability, insufficient range of radio communication (coupled with a high level of noise), excessive forces on the control stick and inadequate range. The latter shortcoming could be eliminated quickly – the LaGG-3 arrived at the test site equipped with two drop tanks.

LaGG-3 with ramjet boosters

A single LaGG-3 M-105PF built in 1942 was modified by installing VRD-1 ramjet boosters designed by Mikhail M. Bondaryuk under the wings immediately outboard of the main gear units (VRD = *vozdooshno-reaktivnyy dvigatel'* – air-breathing jet engine). No details are known as to the fighter's performance.

LaGG-3 M-107 development aircraft

Intent on saving his fighter, Lavochkin believed that the main task was to uprate its engine. He placed his bets on the M-107 experimental engine designed by Vladimir Yakovlevich Klimov. Its initial versions developed 1,400 hp at take-off and 1,300 hp at the second critical altitude of 5,000 m (16,400 ft), thus being 25 per cent more powerful than the M-105P and retaining their rated power at higher altitude.

The LaGG-3 M-107 was built very quickly and entered flight tests, but test pilot G. Mischchenko stated with regret that the desired result had not been achieved. The fighter made 33 emergency landings in 33 flights (!), mainly due to overheating of the new engine. When engine speed was decreased and supercharging reduced for normal flights, the M-107's power fell and all of its advantages vanished. As a precaution, another option had been prepared – a LaGG-3 with the Shvetsov M-82 radial. Lavochkin was very sceptical about the possibility of successfully installing this powerful engine, especially in the short time available. To his surprise, these efforts proved successful, resulting in the famous La-5 which is described later.

In July 1942 the first La-5s rolled off the line at Aircraft Plant No. 21, but the number of LaGGs already on the production line was so great that their assembly continued until the

Above: The third production Leningrad-built LaGG-3 was retrofitted with the Sh-37 engine-mounted 37-mm cannon as the prototype of the K-37 version.

end of 1942. Alterations were introduced in different production batches. In June the use of drop tanks on the LaGG-3 was abandoned and the capacity of the main fuel tanks was increased. The armament of the LaGGs was supplemented by bomb racks. Fighter-bombers were expected to stop the enemy's advancing mechanised infantry units.

Successful attempts by Klimov to uprate the M-105P engine did not escape Lavochkin's attention. Like the Yaks, his fighters received the more powerful M-105PF. Tests of a LaGG-3 from the 29th batch showed that the fighter weighing 3,160 kg (6,966 lb) attained a speed of 507 km/h (315 mph) at sea level and 573 km/h at 4,200 m (13,779 ft).

K-37

Following the trials of the LaGG-3 from the 29th production batch, a LaGG-3 fitted with Boris Shpitalnyy's 37-mm (1.45 calibre) Sh-37 cannon firing through the propeller hub passed tests at NII VVS; some sources refer to this aircraft as the K-37. At a gross take-off weight of 3,363 kg (7,414 lb) the fighter's maximum speed decreased by 5 to 7 km/h (3.1 to 4.3 mph), and its climb rate and ceiling were lower. But, thanks to the automatic slats, the handling qualities were not inferior to those of the previous types. Testing showed that the powerful cannon had a high kill probability against lightly armoured targets at a range of 300 to 400 m (984 to 1,312 ft).

As early as July 1941 People's Commissar of Weapons Dmitriy F. Oostinov signed an order authorising the construction of a batch

This aircraft was used to test the Nudel'man/Sooranov NS-37 engine-mounted cannon installation, becoming the prototype of the LaGG-3-37 version.

Another view of the LaGG-3-37 prototype. Unlike the version armed with Shpital'nyy's cannon (sometimes called K-37), the LaGG-3-37 achieved production status.

of Sh-37 cannons for operational trials. Twenty of these were installed in LaGG-3s, and in early 1942 these aircraft joined the 42nd IAP commanded by Col Fyodor Shinkarenko for operational evaluation on the Bryansk Front. The very first combat engagement proved a success, three enemy bombers being shot down. It was noted, however, that the cannon's 20-round ammunition supply was insufficient.

More combat experience with the K-37 was gained in September 1942 during the Battle of Stalingrad. Despite the fact that Luftwaffe pilots in this region were especially skilled, the results of K-37 missions flown by the pilots of the 291st IAP were even more impressive. In a report dated 31st October

1942, A. Ootin, commander of the 220th Fighter Air Division (to which the 291st IAP was assigned), stated: *'The LaGG-3-37 fighter (sic) is a powerful and effective means of destroying enemy bombers. [...] One or two shells hitting any part of an enemy aircraft are sufficient to bring it down.'* During operational trials, pilots of the 291st IAP shot down 13 German bombers for the loss of seven of their own aircraft. This relatively low LaGG-3 attrition rate was due to the cover provided by faster Yak fighters.

LaGG-3-37

In the meantime, State acceptance trials and flight tests of the 37-mm Nudel'man/ Sooranov NS-37 cannon on the LaGG-3 were suc-

cessfully completed in March 1942. In comparison with the Sh-37 cannon the new weapon was lighter and more reliable. This prompted the government to cancel Sh-37 production in favour of the NS-37. The first batch of LaGG-3s with the NS-37 was built in December 1942. Some of the fighters so equipped (known as LaGG-3-37s) went to the famous Normandie-Niémen fighter regiment staffed by expatriate French pilots.

Initiation of the LaGG-3 production at Taganrog aircraft factory No. 31 under Vladimir Gorboonov's direction was beset with troubles. The plant had barely overcome them and reached a stable tempo of deliveries to the front when the German offensive forced an urgent evacuation to Tbilisi, the Georgian capital. There the enterprise had to undergo a difficult process of unification with a local plant. The difficulties were further aggravated in April-May 1942, when the news came that production of the LaGG-3 at the main plant in Gor'kiy was about to end. The Novosibirsk aircraft factory switched to Yak-7A production, and LaGG-3 manufacture at Plant No. 23, which had been evacuated from Leningrad into inner Russia, was not resumed. Thus, the Tbilisi plant was now the sole manufacturer of the LaGG-3.

Lightened LaGG-3 development aircraft (Gorboonov G-43 et al)

Semyon Lavochkin had long been aware of the need to drastically lighten the aircraft. As early as 13th September 1941 he submitted his proposals to the People's Commissariat of Aircraft Industry. In the opinion of the Chief designer, a possible weight saving of at least 75 to 100 kg (165 to 220 lb) could be achieved by deleting unnecessary equipment items, thereby also simplifying production. Lavochkin believed that the main armament should comprise a ShVAK-20 cannon and two UBS-12.7 heavy machine-guns, while the ShKAS-7.62 machine-guns should be deleted.

After the cessation of LaGG-3 production in Gor'kiy Vladimir P. Gorboonov was given a far greater degree of freedom in his work aimed at improving production machines. This work resulted in a modification offering lower gross take-off weight and better controllability. The weight reduction was due, in part, to dispensing with the all too liberal use of adhesive on production machines.

Gorboonov submitted the first lightened LaGG-3 (c/n 2444) for State acceptance trials. Its gross take-off weight was only 2,865 kg (6,316lb), 200 kg (440 lb) less than that of a standard aircraft manufactured at Plant No. 21. The lightweight LaGG displayed an increased rate of climb and improved manoeuvrability in the vertical plane – however, without any increase in maximum speed

Vladimir Gorboonov's attempts to refine the LaGG-3 resulted in the I-105. This is the first prototype known as the I-105-1; the streamlined nose profile is due to the relocation of the oil coolers to the wing roots.

which was still 564 km/h (350.4 mph) at 3,900 m (12,795 ft).

The next prototype built at Plant No. 31 offered still better results. Besides being lightened, it incorporated some aerodynamic refinements: a retractable tailwheel, an internal aerial housed in the fuselage, removal of the provision to carry bombs, the deletion of additional main gear doors in favour of enlarged main doors, and removal of the aileron balances. Unofficially known as the **G-43** (Gorboonov-43), the fighter reached 550 km/h (341.7 mph) at sea level and 605 km/h (375.9 mph) at 3,800 m (12,467 ft), climbed to 5,000 m (16,400 ft) in 5.1 minutes, and its turning time was reduced to 16-18 seconds. This data was gathered in April 1943.

Production fighters were improving, too, as witnessed by the results of tests that same April 1943. By sealing the manufacturing joints on the fuselage, the cockpit canopy and the engine cowling the top speed was increased to 570 km/h (354 mph) at altitude and 530 km/h (329 mph) at sea level. Stability, manoeuvrability and handling also improved considerably, partly due to the introduction of leading-edge slats.

The steadily improving quality of production LaGGs was corroborated by checkout trials conducted at LII in 1943, which involved nine machines. The results of the tests led to the conclusion that there was a tendency towards a steady reduction of the gross take-off weight – sometimes even to the detriment of strength.

During the three years of production 6,528 LaGG-3s were built, including 2,550 manufactured by Plant No. 31. The last production LaGGs had uprated VK-105PF-2 engines, fibre fuel tanks and other improvements. During 1943 and 1944 LaGG fighters

Above: The forward fuselage of the second prototype designated I-105-2. Note the propeller blade root cuffs intended to maximise propeller thrust and the multiple faired exhaust stubs of the M-105PF-2.

Three-quarters rear view of the I-105-2 ('02 White'), showing to advantage the bubble canopy. Note the inscription '105-2' on the fin.

Above: LaGG-3s undergoing repairs at one of the aircraft overhaul plants, with Tupolev SB bombers and a Lisunov Li-2 transport visible beyond.

LaGG-3s lined up at an airfield, with a very late Tbilisi-built example in the foreground (note the angular windshield). The aircraft wears late-style high-visibility national insignia outlined in white and what appears to be unit markings on the tail; note also the white stripes on the propeller blades.

were used intensively by the 4th Air Army and the air arm of the Black Sea Fleet. According to service pilots, the aircraft was easy to handle and maintain but the handling became heavy at speeds exceeding 400 km/h (248 mph). Combat reports noted its low survivability on ground attack missions and low firepower, insufficient for downing the heavily armoured Heinkel He 111H bombers.

Most of the LaGG-3s manufactured in 1943 went to the Air Force of the North Caucasian Front and to the 4th Air Army where it was the most numerous fighter type.

LaGG-3UTI

A two-seat trainer version of the LaGG-3 designated LaGG-3UTI (oo*cheb*no-treni*rovoch*nyy istre*bitel'* – fighter trainer) was developed to facilitate conversion to the type. Only two prototypes existed; the first of these crashed during manufacturer's flight tests, killing test pilot Popovich. Though not built in quantity, the LaGG-3UTI evolved into the production La-5UTI described separately.

Gorboonov I-105 fighter prototypes

The Design Bureau led by Vladimir P. Gorboonov also proceeded with the development of fighter prototypes. A major redesign of the LaGG-3 resulted in the I-105 (Type '105') fighter, the first prototype of which was built in May 1943. Outwardly it differed from

Above: This late-production LaGG coded '57 White' made a belly landing and is seen here after recovery with the wings and horizontal tail removed.

the predecessor mainly in having a cut-away fuselage decking and a teardrop-shaped cockpit canopy to improve rearward vision. The engine cowling was modified by relocating the oil coolers to the wing roots. The wing slats were deleted – there was no need for them, considering that the gross weight was reduced to 2,749 kg (6,060 lb). The hydraulic system actuating the undercarriage and flaps was replaced by a pneumatic one; the tailwheel was made fully retractable, the radio antenna was buried in the fuselage and the bomb armament was deleted.

The manufacturer's flight tests performed by S. Pligoonov revealed a speed increase of 25 km/h (15.5mph) compared with production fighters (also manufactured in May 1943). In some respects the new fighter's performance was close to the highest recorded in the Soviet Union at the time. This was true for a turning time of 16 seconds, a climb time to 5,000 m (16,404 ft) of 4.7 minutes and an altitude gain of 1,350 m (4,429 ft) during a combat turn. Shevelyov, a 4th Air Army pilot who flew evaluation tests, reported that the I-105 was superior to all Messerschmitt variants in

A late-production LaGG-3 camouflaged with cut-down fir trees is refuelled at a forward airfield.

terms of trouble-free handling and manoeuvrability. He urged that the fighter be put through State tests and launched into production as soon as possible.

By then assembly of the improved second prototype, the '105-2', also called *dooblyor* (literally 'understudy', ie, second prototype, in Soviet terminology of the time), was under way at Plant No. 31. The machine differed from its predecessor in having a Klimov M-105PF-2 engine (the '-2' means 'uprated for the second time') with a take-off rating of 1,240 hp versus the 1,210 hp of the M-105PF. The *dooblyor*'s propeller had blades with airfoil-shaped root cuffs to improve efficiency. The '105-2' also featured enhanced armament consisting of a 23-mm VYa cannon and a 12.7-mm UBS machine-gun.

The programme suffered delays, and the '105-2' was not rolled out until February 1944. It underwent its State acceptance trials at NII VVS from May to June, and the high performance claimed by the manufacturer was not confirmed by the test results: at a gross take-off weight of 2,875 kg (6,338 lb) the fighter attained a maximum speed of 554 km/h (334mph) at sea level and 618 km/h (384 mph) at the altitude of 3,400 m (11,154 ft); it took the fighter 4.8 minutes to reach an altitude of 5,000m (16,400 ft). Ivan M. Dziuba, the NII VVS test pilot who flew the '105-2' during its trials, noted: 'In terms of maximum speed and climb rate the '105-2' is inferior to the Yak-1M dooblyor tested at the NII in October 1943 … because of oil and water overheating, level flight at maximum speed can be sustained for only three or four minutes'.

The aircraft failed its state tests and the LaGG-3 modernisation programme was cancelled, the Tbilisi Aircraft Plant No. 31 switching to production of the Yak-3.

LaGG-3 in action

As already mentioned, the 19th IAP was the first Red Army Air Force unit to re-equip with the LaGG-3, taking delivery of Leningrad-built fighters. However, it was Gor'kiy-built LaGG-3s that were the first to encounter enemy aircraft in the sky. The airmen of the 33rd IAP took delivery of these fighters in August 1941. Led by their commander Major N. Akoolin, these pilots took part in the fighting near Viaz'ma within the ranks of the 43rd Air Division. The regiment took part in strafing missions more often than other units, attacking enemy tank convoys and infantry columns advancing towards Moscow. The powerful armament of these fighters enabled them to destroy not less than 120 tanks and motor vehicles on the road between Dookhovschina and Yartsevo within a few days.

The 21st IAP was next to join the action as a LaGG-3 operator. Thanks to the previously accumulated combat experience the unit's pilots managed to convert to the type within a mere 23 days right at the frontlines, without redeploying to bases in the rear. The regiment was immediately flung into the fray. Among the first pleasant surprises was the LaGGs' high resistance to combat damage. One of the fighters came back from a combat sortie with 75 holes pierced by bullets and shells. Some of the bullets struck the windshield and the instrument panel, shattering them completely. Yet, one day later the aircraft was operational again.

In the course of six days in October 1941 the pilots of the 21st IAP shot down 23 enemy aircraft for the loss of only seven of their own. These machines displayed to advantage their excellent combat qualities not only during strafing missions but also when attacking enemy bombers. Nevertheless, the pilots reported that it was extremely difficult for them to engage enemy fighters. Above all, the LaGG-3 possessed insufficient manoeuvrability and rate of climb. For this reason the 33rd IAP lost nearly half of its inventory near Viaz'ma on 23rd September 1941.

In early May 1942 the LaGG-3 was the Red Army Air Force's most widely used fighter, comprising a third of the total number of fighters in use.

The Nazi advance in the summer of 1942 was a terrible ordeal for the Red Army; the Soviet losses grew considerably. LaGG-3 pilots were no exception. Pilots became painfully aware that the fighter's cooling system was vulnerable, the slightest damage to it rendering the fighter inoperative. The aircraft also proved ill-suited for protecting strike aircraft owing to its poor acceleration; LaGG-3s escorting Il'yushin IL-2 attack aircraft often fell prey to Messerschmitts when attacked at high speed. This, together with the manufacturing defects, earned the fighter a bad reputation; pilots mockingly deciphered the LaGG abbreviation as *lakirovannyy garanteerovannyy grob* (varnished guaranteed coffin)!

The 9th Guards Fighter Air Regiment involved in the operations on the south flank showed better combat results than other reg-

Top and above: The Finnish Air Force operated three captured LaGG-3, including LG-3.

iments, but even this unit, which began flying combat missions on the LaGG-3 in June, quickly lost six aircraft, Hero of the Soviet Union A. Yelokhin being among those killed. Faith in the new fighter was shaken.

Major L. Shestakov, the regiment's commanding officer, analysed the causes of the losses. Being a thoughtful teacher (as well as an excellent pilot), he devised a 'battle formula' to counter Luftwaffe aces. This entailed breaking up the combat formation and flying at different altitudes to strip the Bf 109F of its main advantage in the vertical manoeuvre. Victories were not long in coming.

An example of bravery was shown by captain Voitanik, a 440th IAP pilot. On 2nd August 1942 a flight of four LaGGs was attacked by German fighters near Klet'. Finding himself surrounded by Bf 109s, Voitanik rammed one of his adversaries in a head-on attack and was thrown clear of the aircraft by the impact, parachuting to safety. His action caused turmoil in the German formation and three more Bf 109s were shot down.

However, neither the LaGG-3's high survivability nor the courage of the Soviet pilots could conceal the fact that the aircraft was inferior to the Bf 109F and the later Bf 109G. Its only advantage lay in its horizontal manoeuvrability. Therefore many pilots tended to engage the enemy only in banking turns.

During August 1942 the 440th IAP and the 9th Guards Fighter Regiment of the 268th Fighter Division lost 58 of the 69 LaGGs available. The 273rd and 515th IAPs of the same Division, flying Yak-1s, also suffered high attrition rates, losing 41 of the 71 aircraft in their inventories, but these losses were not so devastating. In late August 1942 the Soviet High Command ruled that the LaGG-3 was not to be used in areas where the Luftwaffe was most active.

Pilots of the 979th IAP led by V. Fedorenko gained fame during the battle of the Kuban'. Being aware of the LaGG-3's poor vertical manoeuvrability, Bf 109 pilots tried to take advantage of this weakness. However, they soon found out – the hard way – that the lightweight Gorboonov-modified LaGGs were quite a match for the German aircraft when flown by experienced pilots. Fedorenko's pilots shot down three Bf 109s with no loss for themselves. A month later Fedorenko was awarded the Hero of the Soviet Union title and the Order of the Gold Star that went with it.

Similar successes were not scored very often. The improved LaGG-3s, too, were generally inferior to the Bf 109G even at medium altitudes, to say nothing of high altitudes. Yet, Soviet pilots who had gained sufficient combat experience fought successfully against the German fighter.

Above: Another view of LaGG-3 LG-1.

Above: Another Finnish LaGG-3; this one is equipped with bomb shackles.
Below: LG-1, the first Finnish LaGG-3, an early-production example. Finnish Air Force fighters wore yellow quick-identification nose markings and fuselage stripes.

LaGGs abroad

Surprisingly, the LaGG-3s were also used in combat by the Soviet pilots' adversaries. Three examples were captured by the Finns after force-landing in enemy territory, repaired and put into service with the Finnish Air Force (*Ilmavoimat*). Serialled LG-1 through LG-3, the machines were in service in 1943-45 with LeLv 32 (Lentolaivue – Air Squadron), going to HLeLv 11 (*Hävittäjälentolaivue* – Fighter Squadron) in 1945. On one occasion a Finnish LaGG-3 even engaged in a dogfight with a Soviet fighter of the same type, neither of the pilots being able to gain the upper hand. Finnish pilots considered the LaGG-3 to be decidedly inferior to the Bf 109G.

A single example of the LaGG-3 fell into Japanese hands when a Soviet pilot in the Far East defected to Manchuria in the spring of 1942, making a wheels-up landing in a ploughed field. In September, after repairs had been effected, the fighter was flown and evaluated by Japanese test pilots who were rather critical of the LaGG-3's performance.

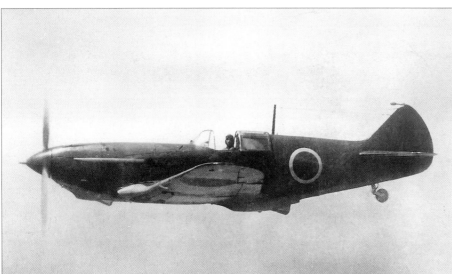

Left above: This early-production LaGG-3 was delivered to the Japanese by a defecting Soviet pilot; note the Hinomaru (Japanese roundels) on the wing undersurface.

Left: The Japanese LaGG-3 in flight. Interestingly, the lower rudder mass balance is missing.

Below: The same aircraft parked between test missions. This example was apparently armed with a ShVAK cannon firing through the propeller hub.

Chapter 2

La-5

A Competent Fighter

LaGG-3 M-82 development aircraft

When the powerful Shvetsov M-82 air-cooled nine-cylinder radial engine became available, the Soviet 'fighter makers' set about designing fighters around this powerplant. Semyon Lavochkin initiated work in this field later than the other Soviet designers. Mikhail Good-kov's Gu-82, the Mikoyan/Gurevich MiG-3 M-82 (aka MiG-9 – the first aircraft to bear this designation) and Aleksandr Yakovlev's Yak-7 M-82 were already flying at the time. On the other hand, all of this work had not resulted in any radical improvements, and none of these fighters had entered series production.

Arkadiy D. Shvetsov, chief designer of the Perm' engine plant No. 19 producing the M-82, was worried by the lack of demand for the engine. Hundreds of M-82s were in storage; only a small number had been installed on Sukhoi Su-2 short-range bombers due to the type's limited production run (it was an offensive weapon but the Soviet Union found itself fighting a defensive war).

Lavochkin's affairs were no better in early 1942. A decision to stop series production of the LaGG-3 was impending. The two designers' troubles brought them together when they met at an NKAP conference in Moscow.

Above: An artist's impression of the La-5 (with appropriate titling on the engine cowling) from the advanced development project documents.

As a result, Shvetsov sent a mock-up of his engine and a team of high-class specialists headed by Ye. Valedinskiy to the Gor'kiy plant in haste.

A task force was formed at Plant No. 21 to design the new fighter. This decision raised an objection from Semyon Alekseyev, the chief of the OKB-21 design bureau, who believed that that the removal of the LaGG-3 from production would occur before the combined team could design, build and test an all-new aircraft. To his mind, therefore, it seemed that all effort and attention should be concentrated on installing the M-82 in the airframe of

Called LaGG-3 M-82, the prototype of the future La-5 was converted from a late-production LaGG-3 airframe (note the rudder horn balance).

Above: The LaGG-3 M-82 as originally flown (with a smooth cowling). The aircraft was only a little shorter than the original version powered by the M-105P.
Below: Three-quarters rear view of the LaGG-3 M-82. The installation of the air-cooled radial engine rendered the ventral water radiator unnecessary.

СЕКРЕТНО

экз. 10 № 258

Above: The LaGG-3 M-82 following modifications; note the large dorsal engine inlet fairing similar in shape to that of the later La-5FN.
Below: The same aircraft with the engine and armament uncowled for maintenance.

10 254

СЕКРЕТНО
ЭКЗ.10 № 232

Above: Most of the LaGG-3 M-82's cowling panels were detached for maintenance, except for the lower two which hinged downwards.

СЕКРЕТНО
ЭКЗ.10 № 233

Another view of the LaGG-3 M-82 'unbuttoned', showing the placement of the ShVAK cannons. The flaps on the sides of the nose with bulges for the exhaust pipes regulated the engine cooling air flow.

СЕКРЕТНО
ЭКЗ.10 № 239

Close-up of the LaGG-3 M-82's gun mount and the breeches of the ShVAK cannons.

a series-produced aircraft. Many thought this suggestion impracticable, as the diameter of the M-82 was 460 mm (18 in) greater than the maximum cross-section of the LaGG-3's fuselage. Besides, the M-82 was 250 kg (551 lb) heavier than the Klimov M-105P, which meant the aircraft's centre of gravity would change. Last, but not least, there was the problem of armament. The production LaGG-3 had a 20-mm ShVAK cannon and a 12.7-mm Berezin synchronised machine-gun. It was impossible to retain this armament on the new aircraft because the M-82's reduction gearbox shaft was not hollow and there was no room for the engine-mounted cannon.

The task was extremely complicated, which is why it was necessary to focus attention of the design bureau team on this work. Alekseyev's proposal was supported by the administration of the production plant and its director, Gostintsev. Among the firm advocates of the idea was K. Slepnyov, the chief of the engine group. Almost the whole weight of the work fell on him and his subordinates.

The peculiar features of the arrangement thus created were as follows. Since the M-82's frontal area was considerably bigger than that of the production LaGG-3's fuselage, a skirting was bonded to both sides of the fuselage's stressed skin. The engine mount was redesigned to take the new engine. Two 20-mm ShVAK synchronised cannon were mounted above the engine. Engine cooling was controlled by two variable outlet flaps on the fuselage sides.

This arrangement caused heated discussions in the bureau, chiefly in connection with the engine cooling system, as radial engines were usually cooled by means of a 'skirt' fitting uniformly round their circumference. Goodkov, the first designer to fit an M-82 engine into a LaGG-3, had done just that. In this case, the powerplant was taken bodily from a Sukhoi Su-2. OKB-301 in Moscow started working on this design in March 1941, but Goodkov was then sidetracked by the need to arm the LaGG-3 with a 37-mm cannon. Nevertheless, development work on a new engine and propeller system continued. In September 1941 the fighter, called **Gu-82**, was flying, and flying quite well. When industrial enterprises were evacuated from Moscow to the eastern regions, Goodkov was directed to Novosibirsk together with his creation.

In late October 1941 the People's Commissariat of the Aircraft Industry was already showing interest in the Gu-82. A go-ahead for series production of the fighter at Gor'kiy, instead of the LaGG-3, was even planned before any tests had commenced. However, the movement of the aircraft from Moscow to Novosibirsk, and then to Gor'kiy took too long, and there was no news from Goodkov.

Meanwhile, the administration of Plant No. 21, not wishing to disturb the LaGG-3 programme, defended their own fighter in every possible way and was not in a hurry to obtain drawings from Goodkov. Aleksandr Yakovlev then intervened, securing a Government decision to have the Yak-7 manufactured in Gor'kiy. Had this decision been put into effect, he would have monopolised fighter design and production in the Soviet Union. Yakovlev was resolute and energetic in his actions. A group of designers was sent, and all the necessary drawings of the improved Yak-7B were handed over. Slowly but surely, Yaks began to oust LaGG-3s from Plant No. 21.

The State Defence Committee's decision in April 1942 to stop LaGG-3 production and transfer the Lavochkin OKB to Plant No. 31 in Tbilisi determined the day when Semyon Lavochkin would be able to demonstrate the best qualities of his new aircraft. At this time the working conditions grew much worse. The government required the first Yak-7B to be assembled in May, and this work could not be hampered. Therefore, Lavochkin and a few remaining like-minded specialists worked almost illegally.

Many events were in store for the designer since February 1942 when his new fighter, designated LaGG-3 M-82, was rolled out. On 14th February Yuriy Stankevich, who had been appointed to undertake the manufacturer's flight tests, was killed while testing a high-speed two-seat LaGG intended for urgent communications flights between Gor'kiy and Moscow. He was succeeded by G. Mischchenko, a Plant No. 21 test pilot, and Lavochkin listened anxiously to his first comments on the fighter: 'The aircraft is good, pleasant to control and responsive, but the cylinder heads get too hot. Measures should be taken'. The first evaluations showed that, compared with the series-production LaGG, the LaGG-3 M-82's speed at ground level was a full 10 per cent greater. The result was brilliant, as great effort was required to get every extra kilometre per hour.

Valedinskiy informed Shvetsov about the first flights immediately. Hoping that at last his engines would be widely used, the latter told N. Goosarov, Secretary of the Perm' Regional Party Committee, of the LaGG-3 M-82. In turn, Goosarov reported the news to Stalin, as did M. Rodionov, the Secretary of the Gor'kiy Regional Party Committee.

Information about the new fighter reached the State Defence Committee in different ways. A report by pilot/engineer A. Nikashin, who had flown the aircraft and backed it enthusiastically, was received there. The voices of NKAP and the Air Force Command were heard in support of the aircraft. This support came at exactly the right time; Lavochkin needed it more than ever before.

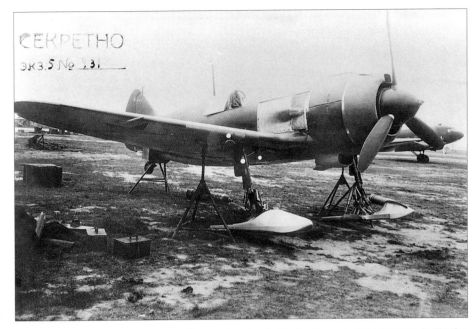

Above: The LaGG-3 M-82 prototype on skis, seen here trestled for landing gear retraction tests. Unlike the stock units fitted to the production LaGG-3, these skis look like slippers!

Above: An early-production 'razorback' La-5. The cowling appears to be painted black.

This early La-5 coded '02 White' is unserviceable, as revealed by the absence of the propeller. As was the case with many operational LaGG-3s, the lower portions of the main gear doors have been removed.

Above: An early La-5 taxies on a grassy airfield. This view shows well the production La-5's rectangular heat-resistant panels aft of the exhaust pipes, the angular windshield replacing the curved LaGG-3 style unit of the prototype, and the bulge on top of the engine cowling.

A La-5 coded '91 White' takes off with the cockpit canopy open; note the white-painted rudder.

A joint commission was urgently formed, visiting the the Gor'kiy plant at the end of April 1942. It included A. Frolov of NII VVS and V. Sabinov of LII, and test pilots A. Koobyshkin (NII VVS) and A. Yakimov (LII) who were to carry out the State acceptance trials, for which only six flying days were allocated. The first flight was made by A. Yakimov on 21st April 1942. He concluded that 'the aircraft is a promising one', but observed that it was very hot in the cockpit. Compared with the flights performed by Mischchenko in the winter, the oil temperature rose appreciably. Urgent development work to improve the engine cooling was carried out.

The State acceptance trials of the LaGG-3 M-82, also called 'Aircraft 37' or 'Type 37', were carried out between 9th May and 14th May 1942, a total of eleven flights being made. They changed the fate of Semyon A. Lavochkin dramatically. On the basis of the test results the fighter was deemed a success and recommended for series production. The performance of the LaGG-3 M-82 was higher than that of all the aircraft in service with the VVS. Its maximum speed ranged from 515 km/h (320 mph) at sea level to 600 km/h (372.8 mph) at the second engine-rated altitude of 6,450 m (21,165 ft). A speed of 560 km/h (347.9 mph) at 600 m (1,970 ft) at the engine's take-off power of 1,700 hp was achieved. A climb to 5,000 m (16,400 ft) took six minutes at normal power rating, and 5.2 minutes augmented. In the important manoeuvre of a climb to 1,100 m (3,610 ft) during a combat turn the aircraft outperformed not only indigenous fighters but also enemy aircraft used at the frontlines. Its range was normal for a single-engined fighter.

The tests also revealed quite a few problems. The handling proved to be even more difficult than that of the LaGG-3 M-105P. Transition from a banked turn in one direction to a banked turn in the other caused stick forces requiring great physical efforts by the pilot. It took 25 seconds to make a banked turn: too long for a single-engine fighter. This was due in part to the LaGG-3 M-82 being overweight, weighing 3,380 kg (7,450 lb).

During the tests the powerplant behaved well, but the lack of forward gills on the engine led to overcooling even in cruising flight. The splattering of the windshield with engine oil, which hampered gun aiming, could not be eliminated. The armament comprising two synchronised ShVAK cannon with 170 rpg was found to be good.

Despite the shortcomings noted above, the flights made by Yakimov and Koobyshkin showed the aircraft to possess excellent performance and acceptable engine cooling. Lavochkin was summoned to Moscow to report to Stalin. He gave a brief and businesslike description of the LaGG-3 M-82, and

Above: This 159th IAP La-5, '66 White', belonged to a squadron named after the famous test pilot Valeriy P. Chkalov, as the legend on the fuselage reveals. Chkalov was a veritable national hero in the USSR.

the new aircraft was backed by People's Commissar of the Aircraft Industry Aleksey Shakhoorin. As a result, the State Defence Committee immediately ordered that Semyon Lavochkin should return to Plant No. 21.

La-5 production fighter (Type 37)

Full-scale development of the La-5, as the aircraft was designated since early September 1942, led to the usual problems associated with launching production. The initial production version had a LaGG-3 style high fuselage spine. The first ten aircraft assembled early in June 1942 were especially difficult to build, since they were manufactured in great haste, with numerous errors as a result. At the same time the tooling was being prepared and the process of producing new components was being mastered.

Aircraft Plant No. 21 handled the task well. The transition to the modified fighter was effected almost without any reduction in the

delivery rate to the Air Force. Following the delivery of the first fully operational La-5 on 20th June 1942, the workers in Gor'kiy turned out another 37 aircraft by the end of the month. In August the plant surpassed the production rate of all the previous months, 148 LaGG-3s being added to 145 new La-5s.

Series-produced aircraft were considerably inferior to the prototype, especially in speed, being some 40 to 50 km/h (24.8 to 31 mph) slower. On the one hand, this is understandable, as the LaGG-3 M-82 prototype lacked the radio antenna, bomb shackles and leading-edge slats fitted to production aircraft. But there were other contributory causes, particularly the engine cowlings which were a loose fit; the air sucked through the cowling joints created additional drag. Work carried out by Professor V. Polinovskiy with the workers of the design bureau of Plant No. 21 allowed the offending openings to be found and eliminated.

A La-5 airframe undergoing static tests.

This page, top and above: This La-5 (c/n 37210514) was one of three Type 37 aircraft used by the Central Aerodynamics and Hydrodynamics Institute, the Flight Research Institute and the Central Institute of Aero Engines to test ways and means of improving the fighter's performance. This aircraft has a redesigned engine inlet with a large dorsal fairing (as later fitted to the La-5FN), plus non-standard main gear doors. Unusually, it features an early LaGG-3 style curved windshield and radio aerial design.

Left: La-5 c/n 37210850, another aircraft used to test the new inlet and other refinements.

Opposite page, top and centre: La-5 '53 White' (c/n 37210853), the third of the aerodynamics development aircraft, featured improved wing/fuselage fairings.

Opposite page, bottom: Another view of La-5 c/n 37210850. The nose shape makes an interesting comparison with '53 White'; note also the difference in oil cooler size and shape.

Above: A late-model 'bubbletop' La-5F (Type 39) manufactured by plant No. 21 on test at NII VVS. Note the original cowling design identical to that of the 'straight' La-5 and the small badges consisting of a Cyrillic 'F' in a circle on the cowling and the rudder.

La-5 with aerodynamic refinements

Service tests of the La-5 revealed many defects. In combat it was inferior to the Messerschmitt Bf 109, but it had great development potential. Semyon Lavochkin was aware of this. Aerodynamic improvements, more engine power, better cockpit visibility, control enhancement and weight reduction were the main aims of the work carried out in late 1942 and early 1943.

To increase maximum level speed, extensive research using three production aircraft was made jointly by the OKB, the Central Aerodynamics and Hydrodynamics Institute named after Nikolay Ye. Zhukovskiy (TsAGI – *Tsentrahl'nyy aero- i ghidrodinamicheskiy institoot*), LII and the Central Institute of Aero Engines (TsIAM – *Tsentrahl'nyy institoot aviatsionnovo motorostroyeniya*).

The principal modifications resulting from this work were as follows. The engine cowling joints were sealed; the shape of the oil cooler duct was improved, the exhaust pipes' cross-section was increased and the tailwheel doors were stiffened. Two of the aircraft involved (c/ns 37210514 and 37210850) featured a new engine inlet with a prominent dorsal fairing running the full length of the cowling. The third aircraft ('53 White', c/n 37210853) retained the standard inlet and small dorsal bulge on the cowling but featured improved wing/fuselage fairings.

The test results showed that speeds equal to those of the LaGG-3 M-82 prototype, which

the series-built aircraft failed to match, could be attained.

La-5F production fighter (Type 37)

Together with the engine builders and engine designer Arkadiy D. Shvetsov, the Lavochkin OKB's workers sought to eliminate the M-82's main deficiencies, namely spark plug failures after five to ten hours' operation, unsatisfactory oil pump capacity and a tendency for the exhaust pipes to burn through. As a result of the measures taken, engine life increased from 100 to 150 hours, and the operating time at augmented power was not limited, allowing pilots to build up supercharger pressure without fearing the consequences. Thus the M-82F engine (*forseerovannyy*, uprated) was

A side view of the same aircraft. Note the exhaust burns on the heat-resistant panels on the fuselage sides. The inscription on the main gear doors reads *Ne vstavat* (No step).

Above: Appearances are deceptive – and so are designations sometimes. La-5F '03 White' manufactured by plant No. 381 in Moscow is powered by an M-82FN engine, despite the designation and the cowling design.

created, and its series production and installation in the Lavochkin fighter began in January 1943. Surprisingly enough, the new version (designated La-5F) did not receive a new factory code, being still referred to as Type 37 at the Gor'kiy aircraft factory. Outwardly such aircraft could be identified by an appropriate badge on the cowling and the rudder – a Cyrillic letter 'F' (Ф) in a circle.

La-5F production fighter (Type 39)

Starting with the ninth production batch (November 1942), the La-5F was given a cut-back dorsal rear fuselage decking and a teardrop canopy with a bulletproof glass panel behind the seat to improve the pilot's view. By analogy with the Republic P-47B and P-47D Thunderbolt, if the original La-5F/Type 37 was a 'razorback', then the La-5F/Type 39 was the 'bubbletop'. Despite persistent demands from service pilots, no bulletproof windshield was provided. This time it was the reverse of the previous situation: the service designation remained the same but the in-house product code was, logically enough, changed to Type 39.

In November 1942 the control column to elevator/ailerons gain was changed in accordance with the Chief Designer's instructions. The shape of the trim tabs was repeatedly altered, the control surfaces were reduced in area, and flap area was increased. These alterations gave a more favourable combination of controllability and agility.

La-5FN fighter (Type 39)

Another promising way of improving the La-5's performance was the installation of an M-82NV engine further uprated by direct fuel injection into the cylinder heads (NV = *neposredstvennyy vprysk*) in place of the carburettor-equipped M-82 and M-82F. The first aircraft powered by the new engine was converted from the second prototype 'bubbletop' La-5F (c/n 39210102) and provisionally designated La-5FNV; this aircraft still had the old-model cowling with just a small bulge on top. Manufacturer's tests showed that the top speed increased to 548 km/h (340.5 mph) at sea level and 619 km/h (384.6 mph) at 5,600 m (18,372 ft) at normal power rating, and the engine was put into series production as the

Another view of La-5F '03 White' at NII VVS during trials.

ASh-82FN. The boost involving both greater rpm and increased supercharger pressure allowed an increase in take-off power from 1,700 to 1,850 hp and in normal power from 1,300 hp at 5,400 m (17,700 ft) to 1,460 hp at 4,650 m (15,255 ft) without ram air supercharging.

From c/n 39210104 onwards the dorsal engine inlet fairing running the full length of the cowling was introduced on the production version designated La-5FN. Serialled '04 White', La-5FN c/n 39210104 was the first fully representative production aircraft, though it was never officially referred to as an *etalon* (standard-setter).

In attacking the problem of reducing the fighter's excessive weight, the designers did not leave a single component unaltered. The wing centre section, the canopy, the landing gear and the powerplant were revised and lightened without detriment to structural strength. The attachment fitting of the landing gear shock struts was welded directly to the front spar, and the shock strut stroke was

Left and upper left: '15 White', another Moscow-built La-5F (c/n 3810515), during checkout trials. The upper picture shows the multi-segment cooling gills regulating the air flow; without them the engine tended to get excessively cold.

Below: This shot of 'bubbletop' La-5Fs (Type 39) on the final assembly line at plant No. 21 in Gor'kiy gives an idea of the scale on which the fighter was built. The leading-edge slats are well visible.

Above and below: La-5 c/n 39210101 during trials. Note the non-standard canopy frame with additional vertical members on the sliding portion and the unusually long aerial mast. The object aft of the seat is probably test equipment.

ЭКЗ.7 № 26

Above and below: The La-5NV development aircraft (c/n 39210102) – the first to be powered by the then-experimental fuel-injected M-82FNV but still retaining the old inlet design. It is seen here during State acceptance trials at NII VVS. Note the teardrop fairing at the base of the aerial mast and the angle of the latter.

Above and below: One of the La-5FN prototypes (then designated La-5FNV) at NII VVS. The aircraft's appearance matches that of production examples. Note the smooth cowling outlet flaps without the bulge for the exhaust pipe; this is because the single large pipe has been replaced with several smaller ones.

ЭКЗ.3 № 89

This page, above: Despite its model-like appearance, this is a real aircraft on a real production line in Gor'kiy. Interestingly, the aircraft already carries a serial, '83 White' (possibly related to the c/n).

Left: Another view of the assembly line at plant No. 21. This was the second of two La-5 assembly lines in Gor'kiy.

Below: The La-5FN pre-delivery flight line at Sormovo airfield, plant No. 21.

Opposite page, top and centre: La-5FN c/n 39210104, the first production-standard aircraft, at NII VVS. Note the original circular badge on the cowling with the Cyrillic letters 'FN' patterned on that of the La-5F. Unusually, there is no star insignia on the tail.

Opposite page, bottom: '57 White', a production La-5FN (c/n 39211257?), during checkout trials at NII VVS. Note the new rhomboid style of the 'FN' badge on the cowling as worn by most aircraft.

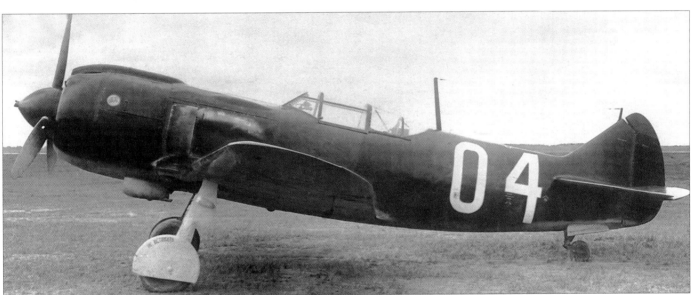

Above: La-5FN c/n 39210109 was used to test various improvements. For instance, the engine inlet was relocated to a ventral position to improve forward visibility, which required the oil cooler to be moved aft to a position beneath the cockpit.

Left: The sideways-opening canopy of La-5 c/n 39210109. The hinged portion incorporated sliding direct vision windows and a strip of steel armour. Note the bulletproof glass panel aft of the seat.

Below left: La-5 c/n 39210109 featured one-piece upward-hinged cowlings replacing the standard double-hinged panels reminiscent of 1920s cars.

increased to improve shock absorption. Changes in the structure of the main spars made it possible to reduce the total weight of the wings. The fuel system was altered to use three fuel tanks instead of five, reducing fuel capacity from 539 to 464 litres (118.5 to 102 Imp. gal.) and eliminating the tanks in the outer wing panels which hampered manoeuvrability.

The first aircraft incorporating all of these changes was sent to NII VVS and LII, where it was tested during December 1942 and January 1943.

The La-5FN's weight was reduced to 3,200 kg (7,054 lb), the dorsal fairing was lower, the cockpit gave a better rearward view and fuel tankage was reduced. One of the synchronised cannon was replaced by a large-calibre synchronised machine-gun.

The test results were outstanding. The aircraft reached 518 km/h (321.8 mph) at sea level at normal power rating, and 556 km/h (345.4 mph) with augmented power (a speed not previously attained by Soviet fighters), 582 km/h (361.6 mph) at 3,600 m (11,811 ft) and 600 km/h (372.8 mph) at 6,300 m (20,669 ft). Manoeuvrability was good; a banked turn was performed in 18 to 19 seconds and the aircraft climbed 1,000 m (3,280 ft) within a combat turn at normal power rating. During the tests the M-82F was augmented at the second supercharger speed for the first time; this increased the maximum speed to 612 km/h (380 mph) at 5,800 m (19,028 ft). The tests could not be completed owing to the supercharger's unsatisfactory operation at the second speed. Besides, test pilot A. Koobyshkin found the structural strength of the lightened La-5 inadequate during diving tests.

The new La-5 bore only a superficial resemblance to the first production fighters. Tests carried out by Plant No. 21 in January and February 1943 confirmed that the speed increase was 30 km/h (18.6 mph) and that all the other performance figures had improved. Even range was not greatly diminished because the weight saving of 150 kg (330 lb) gave the fighter greater endurance, despite its reduced fuel tankage.

A delay in the testing of the La-5 Type 39 did not stop Semyon Lavochkin's work. During March 1943 the OKB completed the second prototype Type 39 (the dooblyor) powered by the already tested M-82FN engine. As distinct from other La-5s, it had metal main spars, like those of the Yak-9. Like the series aircraft, however, it was armed with two synchronised ShVAK SP-20 cannon, and its surface finish and aerodynamics were even better. Pilot A. Nikashin managed to attain a speed of 595 km/h (369.7 mph) at sea level at augmented power, and 648 km/h (402.6 mph) at 6,300 m (20,669 ft). The time to 5,000 m (16,404 ft) was 4.7 minutes at normal power rating. Reduction of the aircraft's weight to 3,168 kg (6,984 lb) enabled it to perform a banked turn at low altitude in 18.5 seconds. Just after these flights the Government issued a decree ordering the aircraft into series production, and requiring that the performance of the second prototype be matched in the production machines.

This was the last occasion when Semyon Lavochkin and A. Nikashin worked together. A skilled pilot and gifted engineer, Nikashin devoted much effort to improving the LaGG and La fighters. In June 1943 he was killed while testing the Gu-1 fighter designed by Mikhail Goodkov.

Unfortunately, not all of the innovations could be incorporated in the series aircraft in the spring of 1943. They had a wing centre section and other components similar to those of series-built La-5s and an all-up weight of 3,305 kg (7,286 lb).

Performance proved to be rather worse than that of La-5 c/n 39210102. The top speed fell to 530 km/h (329.3 mph) at sea level and 610 km/h (379 mph) at 5,800 m (19,028 ft), and climb time to 5,000 m (16,404 ft) was about five minutes – a figure typical of all subsequent La-5FNs.

Manufacturing defects were discovered during the trials. The first production La-5FNs underwent service tests with one of the best Soviet Air Force regiments of the time, the 32nd Guards Air Corps commanded by Hero of the Soviet Union Colonel V. Davidkov. During the battle of Kursk the regiment's pilots flew 25 combat missions on La-5FNs, bringing down 33 enemy aircraft (including 21 Fw 190As) for the loss of six, four fighters being shot down and two crashing during forced landings.

The Soviet aces greatly appreciated the new fighter. Hero of the Soviet Union Captain V. Garanin noted:

'Dogfights were fought at altitudes up to 4,000 m [13,123 ft] with obvious advantages over the Fw 190 and Bf 109, both in speed and in horizontal and vertical manoeuvres. With an open canopy (as Soviet pilots used to fly it) the La-5FN overtakes hostile fighters, albeit slowly, gets on their tails during banked turns, and in a vertical air combat always turns to get above the enemy.'

Shortcomings were also reported. Gun aiming was made more difficult by the presence of the dorsal air intake fairing which could obstruct the target and by the high position of the sight which precluded the possibility of flying with the canopy closed. Pilots claimed that the cockpit was very hot and that exhaust gases entered it, and also that radio communication was inadequate.

The Soviet pilots faced the Focke-Wulf Fw 190A-4s of *Jagdgeschwader* 51 assigned to the Luftwaffe's *Luftflotte* 6, and it is worth comparing the two fighters.

The intention of Kurt Tank, chief designer of Focke-Wulf AG, to provide the Fw 190 with powerful armament and adequate armour protection led to a considerable growth in the all-up weight. The Fw 190A was at least half a ton heavier than the La-5FN. At the same time, in an effort to ensure maximum speed, Tank opted for a rather high wing loading, which degraded field performance and manoeuvrability. Of no small importance was the fact that, while having similar dimensions, displacement, speed and boost, the M-82FN engine offered much greater power than the BMW 801D2 at altitudes up to 4,500 m (14,763 ft). It was at low and medium altitudes that the German fighters were most inferior in speed. Even with the MW 50 methanol/water injection system used on the Fw 190A-4 and the La-5 being flown with its canopy open, the latter had a 15 to 25 km/h (9.3 to 15.5 mph) higher speed up to 3,000 m (9,842 ft) and could get on the enemy's tail after the first combat turn.

Kurt Tank's creation had advantages as well. Its all-metal structure had much higher survivability, and vital components were heavily armoured; the pilot's view, both in

flight and on the ground, was better. A single master control for the powerplant greatly facilitated piloting, and the armament was about three times as powerful. On the whole, however, the comparison was not in the Fw 190's favour.

German experts considered the La-5FN the most dangerous threat on the Eastern front in the summer and autumn of 1943. When one force-landed on enemy territory, it was repaired and extensively tested by the Luftwaffe. The resulting report was clearly intended to reassure German pilots, as the Soviet fighter was described as 'rather primitive' and 'not completely equipped', and as having 'unreliable equipment, a rudimentary sight and a very troublesome hydraulic system.' Concerning the term 'primitive', it would have been more appropriate to use the word 'simple', which is a merit rather than a drawback

The La-5FN was not put into quantity production immediately because the fuel-injected M-82FN engines were not available in the numbers required. Production in sufficient quantities and delivery to Gor'kiy began only in the autumn of 1943.

In November 1943 La-5FN c/n 39210495 was thoroughly tested at NII VVS by test pilot A. Koobyshkin and project engineer V. Alekseyenko. It was stated that the improved aerodynamic elevator balance made the aircraft nicer to fly, but attention was mainly directed at performance. At a weight of 3,322 kg (7,323 lb) the La-5FN developed a speed of 542 km/h (336.7 mph) at sea level (increasing to 563 km/h (356 mph) with augmented power), 607 km/h (377 mph) at 3,250 m (10,662 ft) and 620 km/h (385 mph) at 6,150 m (20,177 ft). Manoeuvrability in both the horizontal and vertical plane was excellent.

It is acknowledged that the La-5FN played an important part in establishing Soviet air superiority and around 1,500 were built by late 1943 when production of this type was discontinued.

La-5TK development aircraft

The Lavochkin OKB also studied high-altitude fighters choosing to use turbosuperchargers to increase service ceiling. Construction of three prototypes fitted with S. Treskin's TK-3 supercharger started in early 1943. One was intended for powerplant development, another for perfecting a pressurised cockpit.

Actually, only one La-5F with the TK-3 was built in the summer of 1943; the aircraft was designated La-5TK (*s toorbokompressorom*). The supercharger increased the service ceiling to 9,500 m (31,168 ft), similar to that of the modified Yak-9PD, but at 3,330 kg (7,341 lb) the La-5F TK-3 was more than half a ton heavier, and its service ceiling was 500 m (1,640 ft) lower as a result.

Above: The La-5 M-71 development aircraft seen during trials. Like La-5FN c/n 39210109, it had a ventral engine inlet and an aft-positioned oil cooler.

This view of the La-5 M-71 makes an interesting comparison with La-5FN c/n 39210109. The larger diameter of the M-71 engine is evident, the thick nose giving the fighter a definitely overweight look.

La-5 M-71 development aircraft

An interesting development was the effort to install the more powerful Shvetsov M-71 engine in the La-5. On this machine the carburettor air intake was relocated to the lower portion of the engine cowling, and dual and triple exhaust pipes were fitted in place of the exhaust collector ring. The oil cooler was moved aft, and improvements were introduced into the fuselage structure, landing gear and engine mounting. The M-71 delivered 2,200 hp at sea level, compared with the M-82FN's 1,850-hp take-off rating. It was also shorter, reducing the aircraft's overall length by 200 mm (7⅞ in).

The La-5 M-71 was test flown by G. Mischchenko between late April and early June 1943. He observed:

'Compared with the standard production La-5, the La-5 powered by the M-71 is less stable longitudinally, which gives it better control sensitivity, easy and pleasant handling, and improved manoeuvrability; landing is simple to perform.'

The aircraft was extensively tested and developed by LII in the autumn of 1943. On the whole, the comments were favourable, and the aircraft's performance was also pleasing. At a weight of 3,526 kg (7,773 lb), which had increased because of a heavier engine, it reached 612 km/h (380 mph) at sea level and 685 km/h (425.6 mph) at 5,500 m (18,000 ft).

The main reasons why the La-5 M-71 was not put into production were the unavailability of the M-71 engine in sufficient numbers and a reluctance to upset the already organised process of La-5 production.

La-5UTI conversion trainer

Another La-5 variant was the La-5UTI conversion trainer which featured a second cockpit for an instructor. The starboard cannon, bulletproof glass, armoured backrest, radio and oxygen equipment, the inert gas pressurization system and the bomb racks were removed.

The La-5UTI prototype was converted from a 'razorback' La-5F and tested at NII VVS by pilots A. Koobyshkin and Yu. Antipov and project engineer V. Alekseyenko in September 1943. It was highly praised and recommended for use by flying schools and reserve air regiments. A small quantity of La-5UTIs was produced in Gor'kiy, 28 being delivered to the Soviet Air Force.

La-5 in action

Series-built aircraft were flung into the fray, and the La-5's combat performance was tested by the 49th Red Banner Fighter Air Regiment of the 1st Air Army. In its first 17 battles the unit destroyed 16 enemy aircraft at the cost of 10 of its own, five pilots being lost. The Soviet

Above: The La-5 M-71 at TsAGI during full-scale wind tunnel tests. The engine has been removed and replaced with a pointed fairing.

Above and below: This La-5 was converted into the La-5TK development aircraft equipped with a TK-3 supercharger. Except for the LaGG-3 style windshield, it was outwardly a standard 'razorback'.

Top and above: The prototype of the La-5UTI trainer was converted at the Gor'kiy aircraft factory from a stock 'razorback' La-5F, as revealed by the upper fuselage contour ahead of the fin. The prototype differed from production examples in having an open cockpit for the instructor. The legend superimposed on the tactical number reads *'Podarok frontu v chest' dvadtsatipyatiletiya VLKSM'* (A gift to the front on occasion of the 25th anniversary of the All-Union Young Communist League).

Below: A production La-5UTI; both cockpits have individual sliding canopies. Note the new-style insignia.

Army command believed that the heavy losses were due to the new aircraft not being fully mastered yet, which meant its operational qualities were not used to full. Pilots noted that, owing to the machine's high weight and insufficient control surface balance, it made more demands upon the flying technique than the LaGG-3 and Yak-1. At the same time, however, the La-5 had an advantage over fighters with liquid-cooled engines, as its two-row radial protected its pilot from frontal attacks. Aircraft survivability increased noticeably as a consequence.

The involvement of La-5s of the 287th Fighter Air Division, commanded by Colonel S. Danilov, Hero of the Soviet Union, in the Battle of Stalingrad was a severe test for the aircraft. Fierce fighting took place over the *Volga* River, and the Luftwaffe was stronger than ever before. The division had its first clash with the enemy on 20th August 1942 with 57 La-5s, of which two-thirds were combat capable. During the first three flying days the 'fives' shot down eight German fighters and three bombers. Seven were lost, including three to 'friendly' anti-aircraft fire.

Subsequently, the division pilots had better luck. There were repeated observations of successful attacks against enemy bombers, of which 57 were destroyed within a month, but the division's own losses were severe, too.

Building on combat experience, the pilots of the 287th Fighter Division/27th Fighter Regiment concluded that their aircraft were inferior to the Bf 109F, to say nothing of the more modern Bf 109G-2, in speed and vertical manoeuvrability. They reported: 'We have to engage only in defensive combat. The enemy is superior in altitude and therefore has a more favourable position from which to attack.'

Hitherto it has often been stated in Soviet and other historical accounts that the La-5 had passed its service tests during the Stalingrad battle in a splendid fashion. In reality, the advanced fighter still had to overcome some teething troubles.

This was confirmed by State tests of a La-5 from the 4th production batch at NII VVS during September and October 1942. At an all-up weight of 3,360 kg (7,407lb) the aircraft attained a maximum speed of 509 km/h (316mph) at sea level at its normal power

Top: This production La-5UTI has a La-5FN-style cowling with a long dorsal intake fairing. Nevertheless, all La-5UTIs were powered by carburettor-equipped M-82F engines.
Above: A rare air-to-air shot of three La-5UTI trainers in formation flight, probably at a flying school. All of them appear to have La-5FN-style cowlings. Note the non-retractable tailwheels.
Below: A La-5UTI with the old-model cowling and 'F' badge at NII VVS during trials.

rating, 535 km/h (332.4 mph) at its augmented rating and 580 km/h at the second engine-rated altitude of 6,250 m (20,505 ft). The Soviet-made M-82 family of engines – derived from the US-designed Wright R-1820 Cyclone – had an augmented power rating only at the first supercharger speed. The aircraft climbed to 5,000 m (16,400 ft) in 6.0 minutes with augmentation. Its armament was similar to that of the prototype. Horizontal manoeuvrability was slightly improved, but in the vertical plane it was decreased. Many defects in design and manufacture had not been corrected.

In combat Soviet pilots flew the La-5 with the canopy open, the cowling side flaps fully open and the tailwheel down, which reduced speed by another 30 to 40 km/h (18.6 to 24.8 mph). As a result, on 25th September 1942 the State Defence Committee issued a directive requiring that the La-5 be lightened and operational characteristics be improved.

The industry produced 1,129 La-5s during the second half of 1942, and these saw action during the counter-offensive by Soviet troops near Stalingrad. Of 289 La-5s in service with the fighter aviation, the majority (180 aircraft)

Above left: A 'razorback' La-5F serialled '100 White' undergoing conversion to a La-5UTI trainer at a repair workshop (the Soviet equivalent of the USAF's 'war weary' P-51 two-seat conversions?).

Left: Probably the same aircraft following conversion; the shape of the rear portion of the canopy makes an interesting comparison with the examples on the preceding page.

Below: 'Razorback' La-5Fs at a forward airfield. The pilots sit in the cockpits, ready to start the engines and scramble at a moment's notice.

were assigned to the forces of the Supreme Command Headquarters Reserve. The Soviet Command was preparing for a general winter offensive and was building up reserves to place in support. One of these strong formations became the 2nd Composite Air Corps under Hero of the Soviet Union, Major-General I. Yeryomenko, the two fighter divisions of which had five regiments equipped with the improved La-5. The new aircraft proved to be 18 to 20 km/h (11 to 12.4 mph) faster than the fighter which had passed State acceptance trials at NII VVS in September and October 1942.

The 2nd Composite Air Corps reliably protected and supported the counter-offensive by troops along the main lines of advance, flying over 8,000 missions and shooting down 353 enemy aircraft from 19th November 1942 to 2nd February 1943.

Progress made in combat by the Air Corps' aviators in cooperation with joint forces during offensive operations on the Stalingrad and Southern fronts were noted by the ground forces Command. General Rodion

Above right: This 159th IAP La-5FN flown by Captain P. Ya Likhoplyotov bears the legend '*Za Vas'ka i Zhoru*' (For Vasyok and Zhora – informal forms of the names Vasiliy and Gheorgiy) to signify the pilot's will to avenge buddies killed in action.

Right: Ivan Nikitovich Kozhedoob, the future top-scoring Soviet ace, stands beside a brand-new La-5FN paid for by donations from collective farm worker Vasiliy Viktorovich Konev, with an appropriate inscription on the fuselage side.

Below: La-5s or early-production La-5Fs taxi out on a mission on a snow-covered airfield.

Above: '185 White', a La-5FN with squadron markings on the tail, escorts another aircraft. The La-5 was usually flown with the canopy at least half open for better visibility. Note the extended tailwheel.

Two flights of 'bubbletop' La-5Fs en route to the area they are to protect.

Above: La-5FNs rest between sorties on a grass airfield.

Ya. Malinovskiy, commander of the 2nd Guards Army (later Defence Minister), wrote:

'The active warfare of the fighter units of the 2nd Composite Air Corps (80 per cent of its aircraft were La-5s), by covering and supporting combat formations of army troops, actually helped to protect the army from the enemy air attacks. The pilots displayed courage, heroism and valour on the battlefield. When the Air Corps fighters appeared the hostile aircraft avoided battle.'

The improved La-5FN was introduced on all fronts during the Soviet winter counter-offensive of 1942-43. The 215th Fighter Air Division commanded by Lieutenant General G. Kravchenko, twice declared Hero of the Soviet Union, gained complete familiarity with their La-5s before running the Leningrad blockade. From 6th January to 26th February 1943 the 215th flew 1,761 missions, shooting down 103 enemy aircraft; the 2nd Guards Fighter Air Corps under Col. Ye. Kondrat did

particularly well. On the debit side, 26 pilots were lost.

Aware of the La-5FN's high performance, the German pilots refused to tangle with them at medium altitudes, trying either to draw them higher or to attack them in a high-speed dive.

The 4th Guards Fighter Air Corps of the Red banner Baltic Fleet was converting from the Polikarpov I-16 to the La-5 in April 1943. Although the pilots and their commander,

A squadron of La-5FNs runs up their engines on a winter day. The concrete hardstand is noteworthy; this is definitely not the factory airfield, considering the dented cowling of the nearest aircraft. The La-5 still featured a Hucks starter dog on the propeller spinner but it was eliminated on later designs.

Top and above: This La-5FN captured by the Germans was evaluated at the Luftwaffe's Erprobungsstelle (Flight Test Centre) Rechlin. Note the lack of the lower portions of the main gear doors.

Major V. Goloobev, considered the La-5 a modern fighter capable of matching the Bf 109 and Focke-Wulf Fw 190A in speed, they became aware of its disadvantages: a propensity to turn sharply to the right during take-off, difficulties in taxiing on soft ground and a tendency for the engine to overheat during ground running. When large numbers of La-5s began to enter service in early 1943, the failure rate was three times as great as those of other fighters. Urgent measures were required to improve reliability.

Some comment is required regarding the La-5's survivability. The use of self-sealing fuel tanks and an inert gas pressurization system in two areas, and, of course, the use of a highly survivable air-cooled engine placed the aircraft in a good light compared with LaGG-3s and the Yaks. However, not until early 1943 were radical improvements achieved. The introduction of bigger centre section fuel tanks (which relieved the wings of their hazardous fuel load) and the drastic shortening of the fuel and oil lines resulted in

a reduction in combat losses, especially during ground-attack sorties.

In the spring of 1943 the La-5 was not inferior to its opponents with regard to combined flying qualities. At that time Plant No. 21 was delivering 350 to 400 La-5s to the front-line units per month, and Plant No. 99 in Ulan-Ude and Plant No. 381 in Moscow also started assembling the type.

On 1st July the forces in the field had 978 La-5s and La-5Fs, more than a quarter of all the fighters available. About 200 aircraft powered by M-82FNs were assembled; some of them had already reached the service units. Only 85 needed repair; the rest were combat-ready on the eve of the great battle of the Kursk Bulge.

Among those keeping watch in La-5 cockpits was Ivan N. Kozhedoob of the 240th Fighter Air Corps, unknown at the time but destined to become the greatest Soviet ace.

La-5s abroad

The Soviet Air Force was not the only operator of the La-5FN. The type was on the strength of a fighter regiments within the 1st Czechoslovak Composite Air Division formed in the Soviet Union in June 1944. In September 1944 the regiment flew from the Tri Duby (Three Oaks) airfield behind German lines in support of the Slovak National Uprising. After the war, the division became the nucleus of the new **Czechoslovak Air Force** (CVL – *Ceskoslovenské Vojenské Létectvo*). Lavochkin-equipped units were based in Slovakia. In keeping with Czech practice of the day the aircraft received a local designation, **S-95**, the S denoting *stíhací* [*letoun*] – fighter.

Shortly after the end of the war all CzAF Lavochkins were grounded on the pretext that in bad weather conditions without permanent hangar facilities their structural strength deteriorated badly. They were vindicated after an investigation at the Prague Aviation Research Institute (VZLÚ – *Vlastní zkusební létecky ústav*), and operations resumed until the fighters ran out of service life.

In 1944 the nascent new **Polish Air Force** (PWL – *Polskie Wojsko Lotnicze*) intended to equip some of its units with the La-5FN. However, this decision was soon abandoned in favour of the Yak-9 fighter. The sole La-5FN in Polish service was operated from October 1944 as the personal 'hack' of the commander of the Air Force's Field Maintenance Workshops. Later it was assigned to the Military Pilot Training School and used for training purposes until finally withdrawn from use in mid-1945 (reports of several La-5s and even La-7s having been evaluated in Poland are presumably erroneous).

A post-war shot of a La-5FN in Czechoslovak Air Force markings. Note the bomb shackles.

Chapter 3

La-7

The Last of the Wartime Lavochkins

Steps towards the La-7

In mid-1943 TsAGI continued studies of a possible further improvement of the La-5. Based on extensive wind tunnel tests of the aircraft, a series of measures aimed at aerodynamic improvements were determined. These included complete sealing of the engine cowling, rearrangement of the wing centre section and changes to the oil cooling and exhaust systems. These alterations formed the basis for the second stage of the La-5's improvements (the first stage was effected when the La-5FN appeared).

To prove the effectiveness of its proposals, TsAGI modified La-5FN c/n 39210206 which underwent flight tests at LII between December 1943 and February 1944. These tests fully validated the effectiveness of the improvements suggested by TsAGI. With an engine identical to that installed in the La-5FN and an all-up weight of 3,445 kg (7,594 lb) the new fighter attained a speed of 684 km/h (425 mph) at 6,150 m (20,177 ft) – 64 km/h (39.7 mph) higher than that of the production La-5FN and 36 km/h (22.3 mph) higher than that of the second prototype La-5 Type 39. In terms of speed, La-5 c/n 39210206 was superior to its counterpart with the more powerful Shvetsov M-71 engine up to an altitude of 4,300 m (14,107 ft).

Above and below: La-5FN c/n 39210206 was modified by TsAGI, becoming the aerodynamic prototype of the future La-7. These photos taken on 8th December 1943 show the ventrally located engine inlet, one-piece engine cowling panels and shiny metal strips sealing the cowling joints. The oil cooler is positioned further aft than on La-5FN c/n 392101019 and the fairing has a flatter, more streamlined shape. Note also the absence of the aerial mast, the aerial exiting the fuselage just aft of the canopy.

Semyon Lavochkin followed the work at TsAGI closely. When the government tasked him with creating a standard for the 1944 production aircraft, all of the TsAGI recommendations were taken into account. The aircraft built by Plant No. 21 in Gor'kiy in January 1944

under the leadership of Semyon Alekseyev differed in several important respects from its forebears. Metal wing spars were used instead of wooden ones; the internal and external sealing of the powerplant and airframe was improved, as on La-5 c/n 39210206.

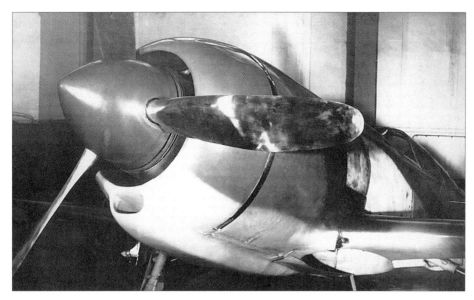

Above: Close-up of the engine cowling and propeller of La-5FN c/n 39210206.

Above: The cowling of La-5FN c/n 39210206 with the cooling air efflux regulating flap removed, showing the six port side exhaust stubs

The oil cooler air intake of La-5FN c/n 39210206.

Three experimental Berezin B-20 synchronised cannon were fitted instead of two cannon. The oil cooler was moved from the bottom of the engine cowling to the centre fuselage underside and housed in a duct of improved aerodynamic configuration. The location and shape of the engine inlet pipe was changed (it was provided with two intakes built into the wing leading edge at the roots instead of one intake placed underneath the engine cowling; this external feature distinguished the *etalon* (production standard-setter aircraft) of 1944 from La-5 c/n 39210206. Other new features were the improved wing/fuselage fillets, individual exhaust pipes for each of the engine cylinders, fewer engine cowling covers, longer landing gear shock struts and a shorter tail strut, the use of a propeller having a Mach-resistant blade airfoil (as already tested on the La-5FN), a metal roll bar in the fixed aft portion of the canopy protecting the pilot in the event of a nose-over, and an updated gunsight.

On completion the aircraft was tested at NII VVS by pilot A. Koobyshkin and project engineer V. Alekseyenko. After a short period of trials, from February to March 1944, the flights were suspended owing to two engine failures. Koobyshkin made only nine flights, but this was sufficient to show that the aircraft was good.

At an all-up weight of 3,265 kg (7,197 lb) the 1944-standard La-5 achieved a speed of 597 km/h (370 mph) at sea level and 680 km/h (422 mph) at 6,000 m (19,685 ft) at normal power rating (there was no time for further tests), while 4.45 minutes were required to climb to 5,000 m (16,404 ft). The test report stated that, in terms of maximum level flying speed and rate of climb, the 1944-standard modified La-5 kept pace with the best modern fighters. It was 50 to 60 km/h (31 to 37 mph) faster than production La-5FNs and came very close to meeting the government's requirements for aircraft of this type. Nearly all of the innovations introduced were recommended for adoption in series-built aircraft. The exception was the B-20 cannon. As its tests were running behind schedule, it was decided to equip the production fighters (designated La-7) with an armament similar to that of the La-5FN.

La-7 production fighter (Type 45)

By the time the La-7 was introduced into production, extensive work had been carried out at the Gor'kiy factory to improve manufacturing technologies. As a result, the number of man-hours required for building production aircraft was more than halved.

Plant No. 21 succeeded in organising production of the La-7 within two or three months. Twenty La-7s rolled off the production line in May 1944, and the first 14 machines passed

Above and below: The first aircraft fully representative of the production La-7 configuration (the so-called *etalon* (standard-setter) of 1944) at NII VVS. The new smooth engine cowling is clearly visible, as is the hefty U-shaped roll bar aft of the pilot's seat.

Above and below: Two more views of the 1944 standard-setter. The side view illustrates well the elegant lines of the La-7; it also shows the new reflector gunsight.

Above: Yet another view of the '1944 standard-setter'; the starboard engine air inlet is clearly visible.

acceptance in the following month. Plant No. 381 in Moscow was even more successful in organising production. There it had been planned that the first five La-7s would likewise be completed in May but they were assembled as early as March, and three had even been accepted by the military. In both cases the setting up of La-7 production did not cause a reduction in total output. The stock of wooden wings in Gor'kiy was so great that the plant continued assembling La-5FNs until October 1944, while the Moscow plant had turned entirely to the improved La-7 by June.

As in previous cases, the performance of series-produced La-7s was inferior to that of the prototype. The maximum speed had fallen to 554 km/h (344 mph) at sea level and 640 km/h (397 mph) at 6,000 m (19,685 ft), which meant that the La-7's speed was not significantly greater than that of a production La-5FN. Although the La-7's weight had fallen to 3,235 kg (7,131 lb), the time to climb to 5,000 m (16,400 ft) was 5.1 minutes.

The reasons behind the loss of speed were analysed by a team headed by Molochayev. The main causes were as follows: departure of the ASh-82FN engine's characteristics from the specifications, incomplete sealing of the engine cowling and fuselage, and deviation of the propeller's airfoil section from the theoretical profile.

With these defects remedied, a production La-7 tested at LII reached 582 km/h (361 mph) at sea level and 674 km/h (418 mph) at 6,000 m (19,685 ft); these figures matched those of the prototype. It only remained to bring production aircraft up to this standard, but this was no easy task, as it turned out. Production aircraft made by Plants No. 21 and No. 381 were flight tested at NII VVS early in September 1944. At a weight of 3,250 kg (7,164 lb) they reached a speed of 572-578 km/h (355.4 to 359 mph) at sea level (or 612 km/h (380 mph) with augmented power), and 655-658 km/h (407-408 mph) at 5,900-6,100 m (19.357-20,013 ft), gaining

Below: The instrument panel of the same aircraft. The placards read: 'Set the flap and u/c control levers neutral immediately after retraction or extension' and 'Oil temp: minimum, 50°; normal, 75°; maximum, 89°.

Above and below: Production La-7s at NII VVS during checkout tests. The production model reverted to the aerial masts of the La-5.

Above and below: '50 White', the 50th Gor'kiy-built La-7 (c/n 45210150), at NII VVS. Note the 'La-7' badges on the nose and tail. Note the difference in oil cooler shape and the redesigned rudder trim tab which does not protrude beyond the rudder trailing edge.

Above and below: La-7 '39 White' (c/n 45210139) at NII VVS. Unlike the La-5 which wore dark green/dark earth camouflage, the La-7 received a two-tone grey camouflage scheme.

Above: Another view of La-7 c/n 45210139; note the exceptionally long pitot.
Below: One more production La-7; the two-tone colouring of the propeller blades is noteworthy.

Above and below: La-7 '77 White' was operated by the Czechoslovak Air Force (CzAF roundels were applied later). The lower photo shows the fighter on display at the Military Museum at Prague-Kbely in carefully restored original markings in company with an Il'yushin IL-2 attack aircraft. Note the fixed tailwheel.

Above and right: La-7 '68 White' (c/n 45214468) was used for development work by the Flight Research Institute (LII). It is seen here in front of one of LII's hangars in Zhukovskiy; note the non-standard frameless curved windshield intended to improve visibility and/or speed, the unusually small star insignia and the early-style LII badge on the fin above the star. Interestingly, the radio aerial and associated masts appear to be missing.

Below: The same aircraft hangared at LII at a later date (judging by the damaged paintwork). The aircraft has been modified into a testbed of some sort, as revealed by the non-standard forked pitot. The radio aerial has been reinstated.

Above: The La-7TK powered by a supercharged M-82. The bulge in the steel heat shield is just discernible aft of the cooling air outlet flap. The aircraft did not progress beyond the trials stage.

1,000-1,230 m (3,280-4,035 ft) in a combat turn, even at normal power rating. This last figure was impressive. Of the Soviet fighters of the day, only the Yakovlev Yak-3 VK-105 PF-2 and Yak-9U VK-107A could compete with the Lavochkin creation which gained 1,400 m (4,600 ft) under augmented power. Various versions of the Messerschmitt Bf 109G, which had hitherto been superior in vertical manoeuvrability, could not match the La-7. In conse-

quence, Luftwaffe pilots had to change their tactics in combat with the Soviet fighter.

A total of 5,753 La-7s was built by three plants (No. 21 in Gor'kiy, No. 99 in Ulan-Ude and No. 381 in Moscow) up to the war's end. Like the 1944 *etalon*, the last of them were fitted with three synchronised B-20 cannon which had been perfected by then. Production of the three-cannon La-7 began in January 1945, and 74 were built during that month.

La-7TK development aircraft

The La-7 formed the basis for numerous versions. One of them was the La-7TK (*s toorbokompressorom* – supercharged). Outwardly it was identical to the standard La-7, except for the bulge in the starboard exhaust heat shield over the supercharger. This aircraft remained in prototype form, and unfortunately next to nothing is known about it.

Another view of the La-7TK. Curiously, the propeller blades and the tailwheel are missing in this view!

Above: The sole La-7M-71. Note the difference in cowling shape with the thicker and more rounded 'lips'.

La-7 M-71 development aircraft

This was another attempt to improve the La-7's performance, this time by installing an M-71 engine. The engine did not enter production, and accordingly the La-7 M-71 remained a one-off.

La-7UTI conversion trainer (Type 46)

Closely comparable with the La-5UTI, a more successful La-7UTI trainer was mass-produced in Gor'kiy under the in-house product code 'Type 46'. The La-7UTI underwent prolonged development, the oil cooler alone being relocated several times. It was equipped with a direction finder and a gun camera; as a result, its all-up weight reached 3,500 kg (7,716 lb), considerably greater than that of the La-7. Still, the La-7UTI's handling differed little from that of the single-seat fighter. The production run totalled 584 aircraft.

The La-7 served as a test-bed for experiments with the first jet engines. With two PVRD-430 ramjet motors under the wings, the La-7 was expected to attain a speed of 800 km/h (497 mph) at 6,000 m (19,685 ft). However, the high drag of the underslung ramjet units prevented it from exceeding 670 km/h (416 mph).

La-7R development aircraft

The La-7R (*reaktivnyy* – literally, jet-powered) was more promising. This experimental aircraft which emerged in late 1944 was fitted with an additional RD-1KhZ liquid-propellant rocket motor designed by Valentin Glooshko, giving 300 kgp (660 lb st) of additional thrust.

Two views of the mixed-power La-7R development aircraft. The rocket motor installation is just discernible at the base of the rudder. Note the La-5FN-style dorsal engine inlet.

Above and below: La-7UTI c/n 46210325 seen at NII VVS during trials. The canopy design is identical to that of the production La-5UTI.

Above and below: The 17th production La-7UTI (c/n 46210117) at NII VVS.

(KhZ stands for *khimicheskoye zazhigahniye* – chemical ignition.) The engine was housed in the rear fuselage, beneath the fin and rudder, the tailplane being slightly raised. The fuel load for the rocket motor was 90 litres (19.8 gallons) of kerosene and 180 litres (39.6 gallons) of nitric acid. To save weight the fuel load for the piston engine was reduced to 215 kg (474 lb), but still the aircraft weighed some 3,500 kg (7,716 lb).

Compared with the La-7, speed increased by 80 km/h (49.7 mph) with the rocket motor operating for 3-3.5 minutes, but the fighter's handling and manoeuvrability deteriorated. During the first three months of 1945 pilots Gheorgiy Shiyanov and A. Davydov made 15 test flights, but not without accident. On 12th May 1945 the rocket motor exploded on the ground; fortunately there were no fatalities. Then there was an in-flight explosion, but Shiyanov managed to land the damaged aircraft. Despite all the difficulties, the La-7R was displayed at a parade at Tushino on 18th August 1946 with its rocket motor running.

The completion of work on the La-7 signified a major milestone in the history of the Lavochkin OKB. It had achieved a considerable

Above left: Semyon A. Lavochkin (second from right) poses with Soviet Naval Air Arm fighter pilots beside a La-7.

Left: A mechanic cleans the oil filters of a La-7 undergoing routine maintenance in the field.

Below: Brand-new La-7s inscribed *Gor'kovskiy rabochiy* (The worker of Gor'kiy) awaiting delivery to the Soviet Air Force.

improvement in production fighters by installing progressively more powerful engines (the Klimov M-105P and M-105PF, Shvetsov M-82 and M-82FN), consistently lightening the structure and enhancing the aerodynamics. While the LaGG-3 does not rank with the best fighters of the initial period of the war, Luftwaffe pilots considered the La-7 one of the most dangerous adversaries on the Eastern front.

The all-up weight rose from the 3,310 kg (7,297 lb) typical of a LaGG-3 in the autumn of 1941 to 3,370 kg (7,429 lb) for the La-7 in March 1946 – an insignificant increase. In contrast, the top speed rose from 462 km/h (287 mph) to 638 km/h (396 mph); an increase of 176 km/h (109.3 mph) at sea level and 100 km/h (62 mph) at 5,000 m (16,400 ft). The time to climb to 5,000 m fell from 8.6 to 4.6 minutes, and climb within a combat turn increased from 500-600 m (1,640-1,970 ft) to 1,400-1,500 m (4,590-4,920 ft) – at augmented power rating, that is. Manoeuvrability did not suffer, as the time required for a banked turn was 20-31 seconds. These were impressive results.

Left: Two Heroes of the Soviet Union, including Major Amet-Khan Sultan (right), discuss flying matters beside the latter's La-7 in 1943 or 1944. Amet-Khan later became a test pilot with LII, losing his life in a flying accident on 1st February 1971. His personal emblem (an eagle superimposed on the solar disc) was later adopted by the Soviet Cosmonaut Detachment.

Below: A La-7 on an airfield in Riga. Note the bomb shackles, the engine inlet covers and the closed cooling inlet flaps.

Above: A typical wartime publicity shot intended to show that the fighting spirit of the Soviet airmen was strong. A group of pilots sits beside a La-7 under the skimpy cover of camouflage netting, enjoying a few minutes' rest and relaxation. The cheerful guy in the middle is obviously telling fish stories!

A La-7 serialled '69 Blue' on display in Leningrad in the post-war years. The fighter wears a uniformly light grey air superiority colour scheme.

Above: A famous aircraft of a famous pilot. La-7 '27 White', the last wartime mount of the top-scoring Soviet WW2 ace Ivan Nikitovich Kozhedoob, is seen here during a brief 'excursion' from the Soviet Air Force Museum in Monino to the airshow at Moscow-Domodedovo airport on 9th July 1967.

Kozhedoob's La-7 displays his score of 62 'kills' stars and the three Gold Star Orders (he was one of very few men to become thrice Hero of the Soviet Union).

La-7 in action

Service tests of the La-7 began in mid-September 1944 and were conducted by the 63rd Guards Fighter Air Corps at the First Baltic Front for one month. Thirty La-7s, mostly built by the Moscow aircraft factory No. 381, were assigned to the tests. All of the pilots had previously flown the La-5 in combat.

During the evaluation period the regiment flew 462 sorties, during which 55 enemy aircraft were shot down for the loss of eight La-7s (half of them were non-combat losses) and three pilots.

All of the accidents resulted from engine failures. One cause for these was the low position of the air intakes resulting in the ingestion of sand and dust into the cylinders.

The combat operations revealed that the La-7's guns had an insufficient weight of fire. A burst of fire was rarely sufficient to bring down an enemy fighter, especially an Fw 190, even though Soviet fighters opened fire at 50-100 m (165-330 ft).

These problems could not overshadow the evident advantages of the new fighter. According to a fighter regiment commander, Colonel Ye. Gorbatiuk (Hero of the Soviet Union), 'the La-7 exhibited unquestionable advantages over German aircraft in multiple air battles'.

Following the 63rd Guards Fighter Air Corps, the 156th Fighter Air Corps of the 4th Air Army began operating the La-7. The flight personnel was very appreciative of the new fighter's operational capabilities.

During October and November 1944 the La-7 began to be widely used on all fronts. Along with Yak-3 VK-105PF-2s and Yak-9U VK-107As, they played an important part in air combat during the closing period of the war. More than 2,000 La-7s, mostly built by Plant No. 21 (the main manufacturer of the type), were delivered to the front-line units up to the war's end.

These aircraft proved troublesome during late October 1944. Six accidents, including four fatal crashes, caused by structural failure of the wings in flight occurred in operational units within a short time and the La-7s had to be grounded pending investigation. The cause was traced to reduced viscosity of the spar material and the defect was remedied. By early 1945 there were 398 La-7s in front-line Air Force units, and 291 were combat ready. This was equivalent to about 6 per cent of all serviceable fighters. By the end of the war this had increased to 15 per cent.

An especially notable part was played by the La-7s of the 2nd, 3rd and 4th Air Armies which were among the best in terms of survivability. A total of 115 La-7s were lost in combat, which amounts to half the number of Yak-3s lost, though the intensity of air combat was similar for both types at the end of the war.

The La-7's high performance became fully apparent in the change of the Luftwaffe tactics at the end of the war. German fighter units re-equipped with the multi-purpose Fw 190A, 'F and 'G used the tactic of 'surprise pirate raids' on a large scale. They would attack advancing Soviet vehicle convoys, the forward edge of the battle area and close rear positions, then escape at full speed, using augmented power. Yak-3s and Yak-9Us had an insufficient margin of speed to intercept the Fw 190s at low altitude, but the task could be performed by the La-7, though not without difficulty.

Ivan Nikitovich Kozhedoob, thrice Hero of the Soviet Union, flew a La-7 until the end of the war. The 17 victories he scored on this aircraft, bringing his total to 62, included a Messerschmitt Me 262 twinjet fighter flown by Luftwaffe ace Colonel Walter Schuck (206 confirmed 'kills'). Kozhedoob's La-7 is now on display at the Central Russian Air Force Museum in Monino.

La-7s abroad

As was the case with the La-5FN, the La-7 equipped a single regiment of the 1st Czechoslovak Composite Air Division and saw action during the Slovak National Uprising. After the war, the type received the Czech designation **S-97**. Like the La-5FN, the La-7 fell victim to the aforementioned grounding order which was subsequently lifted, allowing the type to soldier on until 1950. One example of the La-7 coded '77 White' is preserved as an exhibit of the National Technical Museum, later going to the Military Museum (VM VHÚ – *Vojensky museum Vojenského historického ústavu*) at Prague-Kbely.

The Lavochkin design bureau completed the first stage of its history with the La-7 fighter. Its subsequent piston-engined stablemates – the '126' and '130' prototypes and the production La-9 and La-11 fighters – retained only an external family resemblance with the La-7 and were, in effect, completely new all-metal machines possessing no structural commonality with their predecessor.

A Czechoslovak Air Force La-7 serialled PL-02 on display at an unknown location. The aircraft appears to be painted medium grey overall. Note the DF loop aerial aft of the radio aerial mast. The meaning of the 'ATP' inscription on the main gear doors is unknown

Chapter 4

Tests and Experiments

In Search of New Design Features

'120' fighter prototype

In January 1945 OKB test pilot A. V. Davydov took to the air in the '120' aircraft which became the most radical modification of the production La-7. The aircraft featured a recontoured fuselage and lightened single-spar wings with a laminar-flow airfoil section. To ensure continuity in production methods, the wooden wing skin and wooden rear fuselage were retained. Powered by a 1,900-hp ASh-83 engine, the aircraft reached a speed of 725 km/h (450 mph). However, the engine was still immature, which prevented the '120' fighter from being submitted for State Acceptance trials.

'120R' fighter prototype

The third Lavochkin fighter to be fitted with a liquid-fuel rocket motor installed in the rear fuselage (after the two La-7R prototypes) was a modified '120' prototype which received the designation '120R'. The installation of a rocket booster led to a complete revision of the rear fuselage and vertical tail. The electric battery previously accommodated near the rear fuse-

Above: The thin laminar-flow wings of the '120' prototype were too thin to accommodate the engine inlet ducts completely, hence the bulges on the underside. Note the redesigned canopy with one-piece frameless windscreen and the paint on the forward fuselage sides burned away by the hot exhaust.
Below: Front view of the '120' prototype.

Above: The '120R' mixed-power fighter outwardly differed from the original '120' in having a new, larger vertical tail; note the slit at the base of the rudder above the housing of the rocket booster. The fighter is painted grey overall, with a red spinner and red trim on the engine cowling extending aft into a full-length 'go faster' side flash. Curiously, the tailwheel is either retracted or missing in this view (compare to the picture below), hence the extreme nose-up attitude of the fighter. Unlike the '120 *sans suffixe*', the windshield of the '120R' has an optically flat forward panel.

Below: Ground-running the RD-1KhZ liquid-fuel rocket motor of the '120R' with the cowling removed; the fighter is securely tied down to prevent it from 'running away'.

lage hatch was transferred to the gun mount; the central fuel tank was replaced by a nitric acid tank, the oil tank was moved from the gun mount (where a kerosene tank and an air bottle were accommodated instead) to a position atop the engine gearbox and its capacity was reduced by 5 kg (11 lb). The aircraft's armament now comprised one NS-23 and one B-20 cannon instead of two NS-23s. The ASh-83 engine itself was moved forward by 70 mm (2¾ in). The fuel feed system of the RD-1KhZ liquid-fuel rocket motor installed on the '120R' was identical to that installed on the second example of the La-7R. The '120R' aircraft featuring improved aerodynamics as compared to its predecessors held a promise of making the most effective use of the booster engine.

Flight tests of the '120R' commenced on 2nd July 1945. The first two flights performed on 12th July and 25th September quickly revealed an overheating of the engine oil caused by inefficient design of the oil system, and the aircraft was sent to the workshop for modifications. Meanwhile, the Lavochkin OKB moved to new premises at Plant No. 301, this process entailing further delays. As a result, the '120R' did not resume its flight testing until 12th April 1946. In all, 23 live rocket motor runs were made, five of them with the aircraft airborne. The combustion chamber had logged only 11 minutes and 55 seconds of running when cracks were discovered in it along the burner ring and in the nozzle throat. It was replaced with a new one and on 27th August another live test run of the repaired engine was made. Barely two days later, cracks appeared again during the second test run. On 31st August the work was resumed using the fourth combustion chamber – cracks were revealed after the third run. Finally, on 1st October a combustion chamber made of stainless steel was installed; it showed stable operation during four ignition trials and three live engine runs totalling 50 minutes. In all, the '120R' aircraft performed 16 flights in the course of its flight testing; of these, seven were made with the rocket motor operative. In four flights the starting and functioning of the RD-1KhZ was checked out at the altitudes of 3,000; 2,000; 800 and 70 m (9,840; 6,560; 2,625 and 230 ft respectively). In 1946, during the annual Air Display, the '120R' with test pilot A. V. Davydov at the controls made a pass over Tushino airfield with the rocket motor running.

The maximum speed of the '120R' aircraft with the RD-1KhZ engine turned on could only be measured in one flight. Measurements made at the altitude of 2,150 m (7,050 ft) showed that top speed without the use of the rocket motor was 622 km/h (386 mph), while with the booster ignited it rose to 725 km/h (450 mph). This was equivalent to a speed increase of 103 km/h (64 mph). In all, five combustion chambers were used up during ground and flight testing of the RD-1KhZ and 63 start-ups of the booster were effected, five of them with the aircraft airborne. In all, the combustion chambers logged 28 minutes and 19 seconds of operation. The testing revealed that operating an aircraft fitted with the RD-1KhZ rocket motor was an arduous task which required the development of special ground facilities for filling the aircraft's tanks with nitric acid and kerosene under pressure.

'120' fighter with PVRD-430 ramjets (project)

In March 1946 designers of plant No. 301 evolved an advanced development project (ADP) of Lavochkin's '120' aircraft with two PVRD-430 ramjet engines (*pryamotochnyy vozdooshno-reaktivnyy dvigatel'*) developed by Mikhail M. Bondaryuk and delivering a thrust of 170 kgp (375 lb st) apiece at sea level. However, subsequently the four-cannon '126' fighter was chosen for the installation and flight testing of these boosters.

'124' fighter (project)

At the end of March 1945 Semyon A. Lavochkin endorsed the ADP of the '124' fighter powered by the M-83 engine and armed with three NS-23 cannon, which was also known as Article 'K'. The 'K' was a multipurpose fighter

Above: Though of poor quality, this air-to-air shot is remarkable, being one of very few pictures of the '120R' prototype in flight.

intended both for intercepting bombers and conducting aerial combat with enemy fighters. However, due to the work in hand on more promising projects the aircraft '124' was not built.

The '126' fighter prototype

Taking into account the unreliability of the ASh-83 engine, OKB-301 switched over to projecting the '126' fighter powered by the ASh-82FN engine even as work on the '120' and '124' aircraft was still under way. The aircraft was a further development of the La-7 and '120' fighters. Its wings incorporated a laminar-flow airfoil developed by TsAGI; castings made of *elektron* magnesium alloy were used in various structural units. The armament comprised four NS-23 cannon. Their

weight totalled 152 kg (335 lb), the ammunition supply consisting of 290 rounds weighed 112 kg (247 lb) – ie, was somewhat reduced. The cockpit canopy contours were slightly altered. The aircraft's empty weight and all-up weight remained virtually unchanged.

When designing the '126', considerable success was achieved in reducing the weight of the airframe, which made it possible to provide the aircraft with potent armament at the expense of only a slight increase in the AUW; the La-7 weighed 3,270 kg (7,210 lb), while the weight of the '126' was 3,287 kg (7,248 lb). The saving in airframe weight was achieved by redesigning the fuselage, undercarriage, equipment and some parts of the armament, introducing some rational design features at the same time. Work on improving the wing

The gun mount of the '126' prototype with the cowling removed, showing the four NS-23 cannon.

Above and below: Two views of the '126' prototype during trials; note the bulges over the breeches of the four NS-23 cannon.

structure (single-spar layout with stressed skin and no LE slats) made it possible to obtain laminar-flow wings with thicker skin which weighed not more than the La-7's wings. A considerable weight saving – up to 65 kg (143 lb) – was achieved by using metal instead of wood in the structure of the fuselage and stabiliser. Increasing the calibre and number of cannon gave a greater firepower: the La-7's three UB-20 cannon had a salvo weight of 3.1 kg/sec (6.8 lb/sec), while the '126' fighter's weight of fire was as high as 6.0 kg/sec (13.2 lb/sec). The aircraft's equipment was also subjected to revision, especially in the cockpit which was made more agreeable and comfortable. Provision was made for installing a direction finder on the aircraft.

Manufacturer's tests of the '126' prototype conducted by OKB test pilots A. V. Davydov, Ye. I. Fyodorov and A. A. Popov were completed on 10th January 1945. The aircraft did not enter production, but it became the precursor of the '130' all-metal fighter. Very often, even in NKAP and People's Commissariat of Defence (*Narodnyy komissariaht oborony*) documents, the new machine was referred to as 'the all-metal La-7'.

'164' fighter prototype

When factory testing of the '126' fighter was completed, a decision was taken to equip it with two booster jet engines designed by Mikhail M. Bondaryuk (the PVRD-430 ramjets). The aircraft thus modified received the factory designation '164'. Both outer wing panels were provided with four quick-release attachment points for the boosters, metal fairings were installed between the lower wing surface and the booster engine casing, and a pitot tube was mounted on the left wing outer panel above the booster engine. In addition to this, the stabiliser attachment unit and the elevator spar were reinforced. Equipment items associated with the work of the booster engines were installed in the cockpit. The space previously occupied by two cannon (the port and the outer starboard cannon) and by the ammunition boxes was used to accommodate control and feed units of the booster engine system.

In the period between 26th June and 4th September 1946 joint factory tests of the '164' aircraft were held at the flight-test facility of Plant No. 301. Their purpose was to obtain basic data for determining the efficiency and operational properties of the booster engines. Factory test pilots A. V. Davydov and A. A. Popov made 34 flights (29 and 5 respectively), logging a total of 12.5 hours at altitudes of 200; 500; 1,000; 2,000; 3,000 and 4,800 m (660; 1,640; 3,280; 6,560; 9,840 and 15,750 ft). The ramjet booster engines were turned on in 30 flights; their total time of operation in the air amounted to 46 minutes. The boosters were

Above: Head-on view of the '164' fighter prototype, showing how close the ramjet boosters were located to the main gear units.

turned on 110 times; of these, in 20 cases there were ignition failures caused by malfunctions in the ignition and fuel feed systems. The maximum speed attained with the booster engines running was 694 km/h (431 mph) at the altitude of 2,340 m (7,677 ft) and 663 km/h (412 mph) at 1,235m (4,052 ft). The speed increase was 109 and 104 km/h (67 and 65 mph) respectively, which tallied well with estimated data and bore witness to the proper functioning of the booster engines. However, the boosters created a lot of drag which had a negative effect on the performance. As a result, the speed increase as compared to the aircraft with no boosters amounted to a mere 64 km/h and 62 km/h (39.8mph and 38.5 mph) at the indicated altitudes.

The use of ramjets as booster engines offered a number of advantages compared to liquid-fuel rocket boosters. Less time was required for pre-flight preparations; the boosters ran on the same fuel as the main engine and there were no corrosive substances (such as nitric acid) on board. Finally, the boosters could be repeatedly turned on and off in flight and were easily detachable. In addition to all this, the PVRD-430 booster proved to be very simple in operation and maintenance.

The '164' was not put into series production for several reasons. Firstly, the PVRD-430 engines failed to reach production status and were manufactured only for installation on experimental aircraft. Secondly, testing of new, improved versions of piston-engined fighters demonstrated the feasibility of reaching the speeds attained by the '164' prototype by simpler means, without resorting to the use of mixed powerplants.

Side view of the '164'; once again the fighter was painted medium grey overall with red trim. As these views show, the PVRD-430 boosters were relatively compact units.

Two more views of the '164' during trials. Note the soot stains on the cowling above the engine exhaust ports, apparently caused by firing the cannon.

Chapter 5

The Last of the Kind

Perfecting the Prop-Driven Fighter

'130' and '130D' fighter prototypes

In 1945 the Lavochkin OKB worked on one more fighter in parallel with the '126' machine; it bore the in-house designation Article '130'. Both fighters were of all-metal construction and were structurally identical, except that the former retained plywood wing skins. The wings of the '130' were lightened, which permitted them to accommodate more fuel, enabling the machine to be used as an escort fighter. The armament of both machines comprised a quartet of NS-23 cannon providing a salvo weight of 6 kg/sec (13.2 lb/sec).

The first prototype of the '130' fighter was built in January 1946 at Plant No. 21 which manufactured the La-7. In the following month the machine was moved to Plant No. 301 in Khimki near Moscow. The manufacturer's flight test programme comprised 30 flights and was completed in May 1946 (project pilot A. A. Popov, project engineer L. A. Bal'yan). On 9th June the aircraft was submitted to GK NII VVS (the Red Banner State Air Force Research Institute) for State Acceptance trials. Engineer-pilot V. I. Alekseyenko and test pilot A. G. Koobyshkin were put in charge of

the machine. The very first flights revealed serious defects associated with stability and controllability and the aircraft's armament. On 8th July the machine was returned to the OKB, and it was not until 17 days later that the tests were resumed; they were completed on 10th October with good results. In the course of the trials nearly 45 days were wasted, being spent on changing the engine and adjusting the armament.

It should be noted that the institute not only conducted the testing but undertook development work on the machine as well. Among other things, it was GK NII VVS staff that effected improvements to the control system and achieved a reduction of the stick forces, bringing them to a normal level. The Air Force Research Institute of the succeeded in doing something that had proved beyond the capacity of the OKB. Concurrently, following the recommendations of G. P. Svishchev, the future Academician, the airfoil of the wing centre section was given a more pointed forward part which considerably improved the aircraft's spinning properties.

Besides Alekseyenko and Koobyshkin, the fighter was flown by A. G. Proshakov, V. I. Khomiakov, A. G. Terent'yev, V. P. Trofimov, A. P. Soproon, by Heroes of the Soviet Union I. V. Timofeyenko and V. G. Masich, and by A. G. Kochetkov, Yuriy A. Antipov, L. M. Koovshinov and Gheorgiy A. Sedov who were awarded this high distinction later. The State Acceptance trials report stated:

'As regards range and endurance in the most economical flight mode, the '130' aircraft has a considerable advantage over the La-7, Yak-3 and Yak-9U aircraft. This advantage can be put to good use for the purpose of escorting short-range bombers within their full combat radius, providing a further increase in the fuel capacity is effected.

As far as the weight of fire is concerned, the '130' aircraft is considerably superior to the La-7, Yak-3 and Yak-9U. The '130' aircraft can fulfil its combat missions in daytime at altitudes up to its service ceiling, and in adverse weather conditions as well'.

The '130' prototype had a considerably better view from the cockpit as compared to

The first prototype of the '130' fighter during manufacturer's flight tests.

91

Above and below: Two more views of the first prototype at the manufacturer's flight test stage. Note the bulges over the cannon breeches, the ADF loop aerial under the canopy and the heat-resistant plates around the muzzle orifices. The slender rear fuselage gave something of a tadpole effect.

the German Fw 190 and the American Republic P-47 Thunderbolt fighter. However, along with the fighter's virtues, test pilots noted a total of 117 defects of the aircraft, its equipment and armament. Of these, 17 defects had to be rectified as a matter of priority.

The '130' aircraft had, in fact, very little in common with the La-7. First of all, the new fighter was of all-metal design, which made it possible to reduce the weight of the airframe. The wings were of single-spar stressed-skin construction.

The powerplant consisted of an ASh-82FN engine with a two-speed supercharger driving a VISh-105V-4 three-blade airscrew (*vint izmenyayemovo shahga* – variable-pitch propeller) of 3.1 m (10 ft 2 in) diameter. The all-metal construction of the airframe made it possible to increase the number of fuel tanks to five; their total capacity was 825 litres (181.5 Imp gal). (Later, on production machines, it was increased to 850 litres/187 Imp gal.) The tanks were accommodated in the wing centre section and in the outer wing panels. The centre tank of 270-litre (59.4-gal) capacity was a metal tank with self-sealing coating, the other tanks were flexible fuel cells. The armament comprised four synchronised NS-23 cannon with a total ammunition supply of 300 rounds. The electro-pneumatic fire control system permitted the upper and lower pairs of cannon to be fired separately, or all four weapons to be fired in a salvo. In addition to the standard flight instrumentation, navigation equipment and engine control instruments, the aircraft was fitted with an RSI transmitter and an RSI-6M receiver, an RPKO-10M DF (*rahdiopolukompas*) and an SCh-3M identification friend-or-foe (IFF) transponder ([*otvetchik*] *'svoy-choozhoy'*). An oxygen unit with a 4-litre (0.88-gal) oxygen bottle was provided. A Fairchild Type 6 gun camera was buried in the leading edge of the starboard wing centre section in line with the extended position of the main gear strut.

Attempts were made to rectify many of the shortcomings of the first prototype of the '130' aircraft on the second prototype, designated '130D' (for *dooblyor*, 'understudy'); it was also subjected to the full range of factory tests and State Acceptance trials.

In 1946 the aircraft was put into series production at Plant No. 21, its factory designation being *izdeliye* (article) 48 or Type 48; its official service designation was La-9.

Top: The bulletproof windshield and reflector gun-sight of the '130' fighter. Note the padded chin rest.

Centre: The gun mount with the cowling removed, showing the four NS-23 cannon and their ammo belt guides. The object at the top on the centreline is the engine's oil tank.

Right: Another view of the '130' with the engine and armament uncowled.

Above and below: The second prototype of the '130' fighter (designated '130D') at NII VVS during State acceptance trials. This aircraft incorporated many improvements based on the test results of the first prototype.

Above and below: A production La-9 undergoing trials; note the difference in radio aerial design. The aircraft appears to be painted olive drab with light blue undersurfaces. Interestingly, there is no star insignia on the vertical tail.

La-9 production fighter (Type '48')

The first four production machines were manufactured by the plant in August 1946, but it was not before 20th December that the customer began taking delivery of the fighters. In 1947 the first 30 machines were sent for service trials to the Tyoplyy Stan airfield in the vicinity of Moscow, now no longer in existence (the area is now a residential district on the southern outskirts of the capital).

The aircraft was subjected to constant improvements. In the year of 1948 alone, 197 changes intended to enhance the quality of the machine were introduced into the design. One production machine was fitted with an APSN-44 automatic supercharger speed switching device (*avtomaht pereklyucheniya skorostey nagnetahtelya*); this was later fitted as standard to the improved La-11 fighter.

In the spring of 1949 one La-9 machine was used for testing a device called APPS-TsAGI which was intended to prevent the fighter from entering excessively high G-load flight modes and then entering a spin; the device proved successful and was recommended for installation on production La-9s.

In May 1947 Air Force test pilots A. G. Terent'yev and K. F. Volyntsev conducted checkout tests of two production examples (c/ns 48210410 and 48210425) at GK NII VVS. The testing corroborated previously obtained performance figures, with the exception of range. At an all-up weight of 3,675 kg (8,104 lb) the first of these aircraft was filled with 850 litres (187 Imp gal) of fuel, and the second one with 825 litres (181.5 Imp gal). Technical range in the most economical flight mode (altitude 1,000 m/3,280 ft, indicated airspeed 381 km/h; 237 mph) amounted to 1,995 km (1,240 miles), the endurance being 5 hours 09 minutes (as against 1,735 km/1,078 miles and 4.5 hours for the '130' prototype). High-speed range when flying at an indicated airspeed of 430 km/h (267 mph) at an altitude of 6,000 m (19,680 ft) was 1,060 km (659 miles), the endurance being 3 hours 21 minutes.

From 1947 onwards Plant No. 99 in Ulan-Ude also started manufacturing the La-9. Testing of the first production machine from Ulan-Ude (c/n 01-01) assembled from parts delivered by Plant No. 21 began on 9th July.

In the course of series production which lasted from 1946 to 1948, a total of 1,559 La-9 aircraft was built. Of these, 15 were produced in 1946, 840 in 1947 and 704 in 1948. On production machines the PBP (V) gunsight mounted under the windscreen was replaced by an ASP-1N computing optical sight (*avtomaticheskiy strelkovyy pritsel*). Curiously, the ASP-1N developed by OKB-16 (factory designation 'Article 97-P') was a copy of the British MC-2D gunsight used on Lend-Lease fighters supplied to the USSR during the war.

La-9 fighters were supplied to the Communist China where they opposed USAF and Kuomintang (Republic of China Air Force) aircraft at the beginning of the 1950s. At present several surviving machines are preserved in the collection of the People's Liberation Army Air Force (PLAAF) Museum in Datang Shan, including examples bearing the tactical numbers '06 Red' and '03 Blue'.

Interestingly, the La-9 had a finger in the pie in the creation of the East German Air Force, although it did not fly in EGAF colours. In 1952 five written-off examples of the La-9 were donated by a Soviet unit stationed in East Germany to *Fliegertechnische Schule Kamenz* which trained ground personnel for the so-called *Volkspolizei-Luft* ('People's Police (Air)'), later transformed into *Luftstreitkräfte der Nationale Volksarmee*. The aircraft were used only as ground instructional airframes. Their ultimate fate is unknown.

UTI-La-9 (La-9V, Type '49') conversion trainer

On 18th October 1946 the Soviet Council of Ministers issued directive No. 2339-996 which, among other things, called for the creation of a trainer based on the single-seat '130' fighter. Initially designated La-9V (*vyvoznoy*

A production Gor'kiy-built La-9 at NII VVS. Note the factory's badge on the cowling and the absence of the DF loop under the fixed rear portion of the canopy.

Above and below: A La-9 built by plant No. 99 seen at NII VVS during checkout trials. Unlike the example on the previous page, the DF loop aerial is in place. The engine cooling shutters are fully closed.

Eight Gor'kiy-built La-9s formate with the camera ship in line abreast formation. Interestingly, none of the fighters carries a tactical number. The angular tips of the wings and horizontal tail are readily apparent in this view.

This 'La-9' mounted on a plinth in Nizhniy Novgorod is in fact a crude full-scale model (note the absence of the mainwheel wells!). Basically it looks like a La-9, but the main gear doors are La-7 style, the cowling looks more like the La-5 (but not the blunt spinner) and the right-angle rear portion of the canopy does not resemble anything at all! The legend reads *Rodine ot gor'kovchahn* (To Motherland from the residents of Gor'kiy), showing that the model was built long ago...

Above: This La-9 coded '30 White' is fitted with an indigenous S-13 gun camera in a fairing on top of the cockpit windshield. Note the characteristic curved pattern assumed by the exhaust stains (due to the direction of the airflow around the wing roots) and the red-painted rudder trim tab.

Another operational La-9 equipped with an S-13 gun camera.

[*samolyot*] – familiarization aircraft), such a trainer was speedily developed. It featured a tandem two-seat cockpit provided with a double set of flight, navigation and powerplant instruments and with dual flight and engine controls. Another special feature was the non-retractable tailwheel. The number of fuel tanks was reduced to three; one NS-23 cannon with 100 rounds of ammunition was retained. Additionally, the aircraft was provided with equipment for night flying, with a blind-flying hood in the front cockpit, with a camera for vertical photography, an intercom and target-towing equipment. The two-seater differed from the single-seat aircraft also in having the oil radiator relocated to a place under the engine cowling; it was housed in a rather prominent fairing.

In May 1947 the La-9V passed factory testing, performing eight flights, and State acceptance trials commenced on 2nd June. V. I. Alekseyenko was project engineer and second pilot at this stage of the testing, while

Above right: A typical publicity shot of 'Ye Brave Soviet Airman' standing on the wing of his fighter, scanning the skies for any signs of hostile aircraft attacking his homeland. This view gives a good close-up of the badge on the cowling – a stylised aircraft incorporating the designation (La-9 in Cyrillic) and the words 'Zavod 21' (Plant 21).

Right: This still-unpainted La-9 came to grief during a pre-delivery test flight at the Ulan-Ude aircraft factory. Note the 'storm weights' tying down the rear fuselage.

Below: Soviet Air Force pilots pose before a Gor'kiy-built La-9. The stripes on the tail and the partially red-coloured spinner are unit markings.

Above and below: '01 White', the first prototype of the La-9V (UTI La-9) trainer converted from a Gor'kiy-built single-seater. As compared to the La-5UTI and La-7UTI, the aircraft offered the back-seater rather better visibility. Note the location of the oil cooler.

Above and below: The second prototype of the La-9V. Note the offset position of the aerial mast.

Above and below: A production UTI La-9 (c/n 49990609) at NII VVS during State acceptance trials. Note the S-13 gun camera atop the cockpit windshield.

Above: Another production UTI La-9. This one does not have a gun camera.
Below: Head-on view of UTI La-9 c/n 49990609 at NII VVS.

Above: The trainee's instrument panel of the UTI La-9.

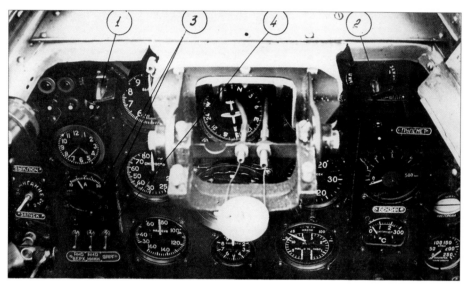

Above: The instructor's instrument panel of the UTI La-9.

The UTI La-9 with the cowling removed, showing the UBS 12.7-mm machine-gun.

I. M. Dziuba was the project test pilot. Like any new machine, the La-9V had its fair share of defects and shortcomings. Nevertheless, the document on the results of the State Acceptance trials stated that '...with regard to its flying qualities and performance, as well as to the equipment fit, the aircraft can be widely used in flying schools and Air Force units as a fighter-trainer for conversion and training of the flying personnel'.

In April 1948 the 'sparka' (a Russian slang term for a trainer, derived from **spah**rennoye oopravl**en**iye – dual controls) entered quantity production at Plant No. 99 in Ulan-Ude under the designation UTI La-9 (or UTILa-9, also known as 'Article 49'). That same year UTI La-9 c/n 49990609 was transferred to GK NII VVS for checkout tests. Upon their completion the aircraft was sent to Plant No. 301 for development work. The cannon installed on the fighter-trainer was replaced by an Berezin UBS-12.7 machine-gun. The ASP-1N gunsight was replaced by an ASP-3N gunsight, new lighting and fire-fighting equipment was installed. The tailwheel was replaced by a new one, of the type used on the La-11 fighter. In this configuration the aircraft passed State Acceptance trials and was recommended for series production. Pilot Pyotr M. Stefanovskiy and engineer-pilot N. I. Sokolov were in charge of the machine. Concluding part of the document on the results of the State acceptance trials stated that 'the use of the UBS machine-gun makes it possible to use the aircraft for training flights involving attacks against both ground and air targets'. It should be borne in mind that using a cannon for this purpose was fraught with a high probability of hitting not only the target drogue but the target-towing aircraft as well.

The factory produced the two-seat fighter-trainers both with the UBS machine-gun and with the NS-23 cannon. In the course of operational service the powerplants of some UTI La-9s were replaced by those taken from the La-11 (which is described below), featuring a neater arrangement of the oil cooler inside the lower part of the engine cowling. Apparently these machines were misidentified by some authors as the 'La-11UTI', a version which never existed.

The two-seat versions of the La-9 were also supplied to China along with the single-seat fighters. One such two-seater has survived and is preserved in the PLAAF museum.

The La-9RD experimental fighter

A production La-9 coded '09 White' (c/n 48210509) was fitted with two RD-13 pulse-jets designed by V. N. Chelomey at Plant No. 51. Known as the La-9RD, the aircraft passed State Acceptance trials in the period between 21st November 1947 and 13th January 1948. Test pilot in charge of the aircraft was I. M.

Dziuba. Modifications to the aircraft included a revised fuel feed system, deletion of the armoured backrest and of two NS-23 cannon and restressing of the airframe. The speed increase amounted to 70 km/h (43.5 mph). The pilot noted strong vibrations and noise when the pulse-jets were turned on. Suspension of the pulse-jets under the wings led to deterioration of manoeuvrability and airfield performance of the aircraft. Start-up of the booster engines was unreliable, endurance dropped sharply, maintenance became much more complicated. The work conducted on this aircraft proved useful only with regard to perfecting pulse-jets intended for installation on cruise missiles.

The pulse-jet equipped aircraft took part in air displays and invariably stunned the public with their thunderous fly-past. According to eye-witness reports, groups numbering from three to nine La-9RD fighters took part in various air displays; this was an impressive sight because the pulse-jet boosters produced an ear-splitting roar. Tests with the pulse-jets reached their culmination in the shape of a fly-past of nine La-9RDs during the Air Display in Tushino in the summer of 1947. The aircraft were flown by GK NII VVS test pilots V. I. Alekseyenko, A. G. Koobyshkin, L. M. Koovshinov, A. P. Manucharov, V. U. Masich, G. A. Sedov, P. M. Stefanovskiy, A. G. Terent'yev and V. P. Trofimov.

The ASP-3N computing gunsight fitted to the UTI La-9 trainer. The sight was designed to work together with NS-23 cannon, as indicated by the inscription on the body.

The La-9RD development aircraft ('09 White', c/n 48210509), seen here without the RD-13 pulse-jet boosters. This picture shows well the large pylons for the boosters protruding far beyond the wing leading edge.

Above and below: The La-9RD with the boosters in place. The RD-13 pulse-jets were quite bulky units, hence the large size of the pylons.

'130R' fighter prototype

In the spring of 1946 construction was started of the '130R' experimental aircraft fitted with an additional liquid-fuel rocket motor. In those years this type of engine, despite its enormous fuel consumption and highly toxic oxidants, was mounted on many fighters. Fitting the RD-1KhZ liquid-fuel rocket motor to this particular machine necessitated considerable changes in its configuration. The central fuel tank was replaced by a nitric acid tank. The actuators of the pumps feeding fuel components to the rocket motor were geared to the ASh-83FN engine. The kerosene tank was placed between the ASh-83FN and the cockpit under the gun mount on which only two cannon were retained. To ensure the proper centre of gravity position the main engine was moved forward by 170.5 mm (6.7 in), which necessitated the manufacture of new engine mounts and cowlings. However, the longitudinal stability margin proved insufficient and the empennage area had to be increased; the fabric covering of the rudder and elevators gave way to metal skinning. The additional weight of the tail unit caused by all these modifications made it necessary to reinforce the tailwheel fork.

Later in 1946, when the assembly of the airframe was already under way, all work on

Above: The La-138 development aircraft makes a high-speed pass during one of the air parades at Moscow-Tushino.

the '130R' project was stopped. The reason for this may have been the successful testing of the first Soviet turbojet-powered aircraft and the generally unsuccessful attempts to install the still immature and dangerous liquid-fuel rocket motors in aircraft of other types.

'132' fighter prototype

Initially the project of the '132' fighter envisaged a modification of a production La-9 on which the ASh-82FN engine was replaced by the more powerful M-93 engine possessing better high-altitude performance. The aircraft was altered to the extent that was necessary

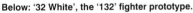

Below: '32 White', the '132' fighter prototype.

Above: The '138' development aircraft under construction at plant No. 301, showing the compact PVRD-430 ramjet boosters.
Below: The same aircraft in completed form during trials.

for the installation of the M-93 engine. The rest of the airframe of the '132' fighter was completely identical to that of La-9. The equipment and armament fit and their placement remained unchanged.

When the prototype of the Article '132' was under construction, the real M-93 engine was still unavailable, so, as a stopgap measure, the aircraft was fitted with an ASh-82FM engine which was an improved version of the production ASh-82FN.

Flight tests of the '132' prototype bearing the tactical number '32 White' commenced in October 1946; then they were suspended, resuming on 7th March 1947. The test programme was completed on 14th April 1948, involving a total of 35 flights. The protracted test period was due to design faults which plagued the prototype engine. In the course of the testing four engine changes had to be made; the engines were used by the engine design bureau for consecutive improvements and modification of various units.

The following results were obtained: maximum speed was 600 km/h (373 mph) at sea level and 713 km/h (443 mph) at the altitude of 7,400 m (24,280 ft). At nominal power the fighter climbed to 5,000 m (16,400 ft) in five minutes; the service ceiling was 11,350 m (37,240 ft). The fighter's technical range was 1,100 km (684 miles). The '132' was submitted for State Acceptance trials to GK NII VVS but did not enter series production because the next prototype aircraft following on its heels – the '134' fighter – possessed better performance.

'132M' fighter project

In parallel with the '132' the Lavochkin OKB started work on the '132M' (*modifitseerovannyy*) fighter. It was to have been powered by an M-82M engine with a corresponding slight decrease in performance; this was an insurance policy in case the M-93 proved a dead duck. Eventually, however, the '132M' project was abandoned.

'138' and '138D' fighter prototypes

Building on the results of the '164' prototype's tests, GK NII VVS recommended that, after rectifying the defects revealed, the '130' aircraft possessing greater fuel capacity should be equipped with PVRD-430 ramjet boosters; after completion of factory tests the aircraft was to be submitted for State Acceptance trials. This is how the prototype construction plan for 1947 came to include the new '138' prototype aircraft. The '138' was a derivative of the production La-9 fighter; it was fitted with two PVRD-430 ramjets, each of which was attached to the wing undersurface by three adjustable fittings. The installation of the booster engines required the removal of the outer starboard cannon together with its

ammunition supply; the fighter was fitted with equipment that was necessary for the maintenance and control of the ramjets.

Two aircraft with ASh-82FN engines and PVRD-430 boosters were built. Designated '138' and '138D' respectively, they underwent manufacturer's flight tests. In all, the first prototype ('138') performed 20 flights, the second aircraft ('138D') making another 38. However, the test missions were successfully fulfilled in just ten flights. In 19 cases the failure to fulfil the objective was due to malfunction of the booster engines. Their reliable operation could only be ensured at altitudes up to 3,000 m (9,840 ft) where the use of the ramjet boosters gave a speed increase of 107-112 km/h (66.5 to 69.6 mph), and compared to the production La-9 at different altitudes – from 45 km/h (28 mph) at 3,000 m (9,840 ft) to nearly 60 km/h (37 mph), although it had been expected that the increase would amount some 70-100 km/h (43-62 mph). However, with the ramjets turned off the speed proved to be 60-80 km/h (37.3 to 44.7 mph) lower than that of the prototype '130' aircraft without boosters. With all engines running the range did not exceed 112 km (70 miles) and endurance was limited to ten minutes. The '138' fighter could wage combat against the US Boeing B-29 and B-50 bombers, also when chasing them, but in a duel with enemy fighters, piston-engined and jet-powered ones alike, it had few chances of success. As a positive fact, it might be noted that a considerable improvement in the high-altitude performance of the mixed powerplant was revealed. However, due to the low reliability of the PVRD-430 engines the work on the '138' aircraft was suspended. It was presumed that the work would be restarted as soon as improved engines running reliably within the whole range of operational altitudes and speeds were made available. But, as it turned out, such engines never appeared.

The '138' was demonstrated to the public during one of the Tushino air fests.

'134' and '134D' fighter prototypes

The concluding part of the document on the results of the '130' fighter prototype's State Acceptance trials stated that '...for the purpose of further enhancing the aircraft's performance, as well as for widening the range missions performed by the aircraft, it is necessary to modify the aircraft with a view to producing an escort fighter capable of escorting bombers, with a range of no less than 2,500 km [1,550 miles] at a speed equal to the bombers' cruising speed'. The mentioned document was endorsed on 18th October 1946 by directive No. 2339-996 issued by the Soviet Council of Ministers. As noted above, the same document stipulated the development of a fighter-trainer, as well as an escort fighter, on the basis of the '130' aircraft.

Both machines were developed in parallel and were submitted for flight testing virtually at the same time. It took the OKB-301 only half a year to create the '134' aircraft, also known as the La-9M (*modifitseerovannyy* – modified). In May 1947 A. G. Kochetkov, a former military test pilot who had left GK NII VVS to work for an MAP enterprise, took the machine to the air for the first time. In the course of 18 flights totalling 12 hours and 37 minutes, measurements were made to determine maximum speeds in level flight and rate of clime at nominal power rating, technical range and endurance.

On 19th June the first machine, serialled '34 White', was turned over to GK NII VVS for State Acceptance trials. The '134' was armed with three NS-23 cannon versus four on the La-9, and the total ammunition supply was reduced to 225 rounds. The oil cooler was moved to the lower part of the engine cowling, resulting in a characteristically bulged cowling bottom, and the capacity of the oil system was increased.

Five days later the second prototype of the '134' arrived at Chkalovskaya airfield where GK NII VVS resided. This was the '134D' (*dooblyor*) which differed in having increased range. Its fuel capacity was increased from 825 litres (181.5 Imp gal) to 1,100 litres (242 Imp gal) by installing supplementary fuel tanks in the outer wing panels. In addition to this, provision was made for the installation of two non-jettisonable tip tanks with a total capacity of 332 litres (73 Imp gal). A. G. Terent'yev and I. V. Timofeyenko were the project test pilots.

The aircraft's increased all-up weight necessitated strengthening of the undercarriage; the main gear legs were provided with 660 x 120 mm (26 x 4.7 in) wheels equipped with high-pressure tyres. The tailwheel strut had a levered suspension. The aircraft was fitted with navigation lights, an AFA-IM aerial camera for vertical photography and an automatic device for regulating the cylinder head temperature.

The increased endurance when escorting bombers (more than seven hours) called for the installation of an additional oxygen bottle and a urinal for the pilot; the seat was fitted with padded adjustable armrests and a broad padded backrest. The normal all-up weight increased by 571 kg (1,260 lb). Despite all the efforts of the aerodynamicists, the retention of the identically rated powerplant made it impossible to fulfil all the specifications stipulated by the Council of Ministers directive. Suffice it to say that the maximum speed at sea level proved to be 25 km/h (15.5 mph) less than specified; at the altitude of 6200 m (20,340 ft) it was 6 km/h (3.7 mph) less than specified.

In the course of the trials, which were completed on 24th July, both machines per-

Above and below: '34 White', the first prototype of the '134' fighter. Note the oil cooler built into the bottom of the cowling, resulting in a characteristic 'smile'.

Above: Front view of the first prototype '134'.
Below: Rear view of the same aircraft. Note the large span of the horizontal tail.

Above and below: The unserialled '134D' (the second prototype) introduced non-jettisonable tip tanks. The cooling gills are fully closed here. Note the black 'anti-soot' panels painted on the fuselage sides.

Above: The '134D' with the tip tanks removed.
Below: The first prototype '134' in flight.

Above: Say 'cheese'! Close-up of the '134' fighter's oil cooler intake.

Above: The gun mount of the '134', seen from the port side.

As this photo shows, the '134' had two cannon to port and one to starboard.

formed 71 flights between them, with a total duration of 59 hours and 13 minutes. On 10th July pilots I. M. Dziuba and V. I. Alekseyenko performed two long-distance flights. One of these was performed in the most economical flight mode along the Chkalovskaya AB – Kazan' – Chkalovskaya AB – Dmitrov – Orekhovo-Zooyevo – Chkalovskaya AB route. The other one was performed at the same altitude but at the speed of 473 km/h (294 mph) from Chkalovskaya to Cheboksary and back again. Technical range was determined on the assumption that two dogfights, each of them lasting 10 to 16 minutes, would take place during the flight along the route (one in the middle of the route and another at the end of the route). The engagement was simulated at the altitudes of 5,000 and 7,500 m (16,400 and 24,600 ft). Both machines were flown by military test pilots Pyotr M. Stefanovskiy, Ivan M. Dziuba, L. M. Koovshinov, D. G. Pikoolenko, V. I. Alekseyenko and V. P. Trofimov. They noted in their reports: *'As regards aerobatics techniques and handling when flown with full fuel load, the aircraft is markedly different from the production La-9'.* In addition to their observations on the discomfort caused by the cockpit interior and controllability faults, Dziuba and Alekseyenko (who had performed the two long-distance flights with a duration of 4 hours 54 minutes and 2 hours 47 minutes respectively) noted, *'Aerial combat at altitudes above 7,000 m [29,970 ft] on this aircraft will be insufficiently effective because the output margin of the powerplant does not ensure the degree of manoeuvrability in the horizontal and vertical planes required for a fighter...'*

Despite the numerous shortcomings of the aircraft in its new version as escort fighter, the concluding part of the document on the results of the State Acceptance trials endorsed by Council of Ministers directive No. 2942-958 dated 22nd August 1947 read: *'The modified La-9 aircraft designed by Comrade Lavochkin and featuring an increased fuel load has passed State Acceptance trials satisfactorily...'.* Obviously, a sharp increase in the range of heavy bombers (in the USSR such a bomber appeared in the shape of the Tu-4 – a copy of the B-29) created an urgent need for a fighter described above.

La-11 production escort fighter (Article '140', Type '51')

In accordance with the abovementioned CofM directive No. 2942-958 the new escort fighter was allocated the designation La-11. It was put into series production at Plant No. 21 in Gor'kiy (now renamed back to Nizhniy Novgorod) with the factory product code 'Type 51', and production continued until 1951. (Here it should be noted that the production version of the '134' aircraft had the in-house designation '140' at OKB-301; this means that the design bureau and production facility designations for the type were not identical – a practice not infrequently occurring in the Soviet aircraft industry.) In 1947 the plant turned out 100 machines, followed by 650 – the greatest number – in 1948. La-11 production was discontinued that year, but in the following year the type was reinstated in production and the plant manufactured an additional 150 machines. In 1950 the output amounted to 150 machines, and a further 182 La-11s were built in 1951. Total production amounted to 1,182 copies and was eventually terminated because jet-powered fighters (which had the La-11 outclassed) were entering large-scale production.

Several months before the beginning of the La-11's flight tests GK NII VVS obtained an example of the Lockheed P-38L-1-LO Lightning twin-engined fighter. Its evaluation, which was completed in April 1947, showed that, despite the Lightning's high all-up weight (almost twice that of the La-11), its range with drop tanks was inferior to that of the Soviet fighter. Other performance figures, with the exception of the radius of turn and service ceiling, were also lower.

Like its predecessor, the production La-11 escort fighter was subjected to a continuous process of refinement. In 1948 alone 210 changes were introduced into the design with a view to perfecting the fighter's operational qualities. The La-11 was delivered not only to Air Force units but to the Air Force's flying schools and to the Naval Air Arm as well. As was the case with the La-9, La-11 fighters were initially equipped with Fairchild gun cameras but subsequently they came to be replaced by Soviet-produced S-13 cameras. The gun camera was located either on the outside of the starboard undercarriage unit or on the cockpit windshield frame.

Even earlier, Plant No.21 started equipping the La-11 with a de-icing system in accordance with a Council of Ministers directive issued in December 1947. This work was conducted in connection with the fact that these fighters were intended, among other things, to be used for defending the Soviet Union's northern frontiers. Between 17th March and 6th April 1948 a La-11 (c/n 51210327) equipped with a de-icing system was subjected to joint tests conducted by the OKB and the Ministry of Aircraft Industry. The de-icing system comprised a device for heating the wing leading edges with hot exhaust gases from the engine, an electro-thermal device for the stabilisers and alcohol de-icing for the propeller and the cockpit windscreen. The wing de-icers functioned satisfactorily but were not recommended into series production because the hot exhaust gases accelerated the corrosion of aluminium alloys used in the wing structure.

Above: The cockpit of the '134' equipped with the ASP-3N gunsight.

Above: The instrument panel of the '134'.

Later on, in the middle of 1948, another La-11 (c/n 51210401) was submitted for State Acceptance trials. It was fitted with BO-20 heaters (*bortovoy obogrevahtel'*) which had been adopted as a standard equipment for jet fighters. De-icers developed for the wing centre section, the fin, the radio aerial and the oil cooler air intake underwent tests almost at the same time.

In the summer of 1951 Plant No. 81 retrofitted a production La-11 with ARO-82 launch rails for rocket projectiles. One machine which was passing tests at GK NII VVS was equipped with an automatic device for switching the supercharger speeds. In 1950 a total of 150 La-11s were retrofitted with RV-2 radio altimeters (*rahdiovysotomer*), MRP marker beacon receivers (***mar**kernyy **rah**diopree-**yom**nik*) and

ARK-5 automatic direction finders (*avtomatich*eskiy *rah*dio**kom**pas). In all probability, not all production machines leaving the factory carried a full complement of radio equipment.

Like its stablemate, the La-9, the type was exported to China. It has proved impossible to find exact information on how many this 'friendly nation' received, but there is evidence that, for example, sixty La-11s were delivered to the People's Liberation Army Air Force pursuant to CofM directive No. 3147-1481 issued on 25th August 1951. Two La-11s are preserved in the PLAAF Museum; one is in Chinese markings and coded '08 Red', while the other carries North Korean Air Force markings and the tactical number '26 Red'. One more La-11 has been sold to the UK and is being restored to airworthy status (!).

Above: The wingtip of a La-11. The elongated recess in the tip fairing is associated with the provisions for installing tip tanks, hence also the position of the navigation lights on the upper and lower surfaces.

Close-up of the La-11's port main gear unit.

La-11 PHOTINT version

An example of the La-11 outfitted as a photo reconnaissance (PHOTINT) aircraft passed its factory tests in July 1950, completing State Acceptance tests on 22nd September of the same year. The machine was equipped with an AFA-BA-40 aerial camera (*aerofotoapparaht*) on a flexible mount. That same year, following an order from the Soviet Air Force, 100 fighters were converted to the PHOTINT version. In reconnaissance configuration fitted with external tanks the La-11 proved to be overweight and underpowered. In 1951 an attempt was made to raise the take-off rating of the ASh-82FN to 2,000 hp, but, as it turned out, considerable changes would have to be introduced into the engine's design to ensure reliable operation and further work on the subject was stopped.

At the fronts of the Cold War

When the La-11 was still under development, an idea cropped up to use this fighter for the defence of the Soviet Union's Arctic regions against unbidden guests. Plans were in hand for deploying the aircraft at airfields in areas to the north of the Arctic Circle and on drifting icefields. This called for a number of experiments associated with the deployment of the La-11s at ice-borne airstrips in the High North.

One of the first expeditions took place in 1948. At that time several scientific expeditions sponsored by the Soviet Academy of Sciences were working in the North Pole area. A decision was taken to send a group of La-11s with the task of performing a landing on an icefield used by scientists. The expedition was headed by Major-General A. A. Kuznetsov, chief of the Main Directorate of the North Sea Route (GU SMP – *Glahvnoye oopravleniye Severnovo morskovo putee*). Catering for the expedition was ensured by the crews of a Lisunov Li-2 transport from the 650th Independent Airlift Regiment, a Douglas C-47 Dakota from the 1st Airlift Regiment of the 2nd Special Mission Air Division and an Il'yushin IL-12D transport from the 708th Special Mission Airlift Regiment. A twin-engined Tu-6 reconnaissance aircraft (a version of the Tu-2 bomber) used as a pathfinder and three La-11s conducted training flights in Arctic conditions, with Cape Schmidt and Wrangel Island as their bases. At first the Tu-6 bomber possessing reasonably good navigation equipment took off from the island of Wrangel for a reconnaissance flight. It landed successfully on an icefield near the North Pole. Then it returned to the 'mainland' and, when a spell of good weather set in, on 7th May 1948 three La-11s accompanied by the Tu-6 pathfinder started on a flight towards the icefield where they made a safe landing. On 8th May, having performed several flights from the icefield, they returned to base. Later, several other similar expeditions were undertaken in different areas of the High North, and only after that the La-11s started performing routine patrol flights for the defence of the Soviet northern frontiers.

To ensure this, a number of technical issues had to be tackled. Among other things, the aircraft had to be fitted with de-icing systems, the navigation equipment had to be improved. Importantly, it was necessary to ensure the possibility of taking off from unprepared snow-covered airstrips.

La-11 fighters of the 1st Fighter Air Division and the 53rd Fighter Air Regiment were involved in the work in the North Pole area at different times. In December 1949 some of the participants of the expedition were awarded the Hero of the Soviet Union title. Among those who received the award were squadron commander V. D. Borovkov and navigator S. A. Skorniakov (group commander) from the 1st Fighter Air Division, as well as deputy CO of the 53rd Fighter Regiment V. A. Popov.

The idea of *ad hoc* airstrips built on floating icefields occupied the minds of the military for quite some time, but none of these airstrips was ever placed on a regular duty for the purpose of conducting combat patrol missions.

The first case when the La-11 fired its guns in anger took place on 8th April 1950. On that day a flight of fighters from the 30th Guards Fighter Air Regiment led by B. Dokin intercepted and destroyed a US Navy reconnaissance aircraft over the Baltic Sea in the

Above: This La-11 was used for some kind of development work at NII VVS, as indicated by the numbers on the propeller blade tips.

vicinity of the Libava naval base. According to some sources, this was a Consolidated RB-24 Privateer. However, the *Izvestiya* newspaper, which later conducted an investigation of the incident, maintains that the US aircraft shot down by the Soviet fighters was a Boeing RB-29. The participants of those events related that the US aircraft had ignored the commands of the Soviet fighters requiring it to head for a landing and opened fire. The fighters returned fire, hitting the target, and the spyplane plunged into the sea, taking the

crew of ten with it. In the same year a pair of Pacific Fleet/88th Guards Fighter Regiment La-11s piloted by I. Lookashov and M. Shchookin intercepted a Lockheed P2V Neptune reconnaissance aircraft.

In 1950 the first La-11s were delivered to China. In the summer of the same year personnel of the recently formed 351st Fighter Regiment equipped with La-11 night fighters started conversion training of Chinese airmen. The regiment was based near Shanghai until the end of 1950; at the beginning of the

For winter operations from tactical airfields the La-11 could be equipped with wooden 'slipper' skis which fell away as soon as the aircraft became airborne. Note the 'La-11' titles on the cowling.

Above: La-11 '02 White' (c/n 51210202) at NII VVS during State acceptance trials.
Below: A production La-11 undergoing checkout trials at NII VVS.

Above: '15 White' was one of several UTI La-9s retrofitted with the complete powerplant of the La-11, giving rise to the erroneous appellation 'UTI La-11'.
Below: This La-11 is probably a late-production example; note the lightened mainwheels with eight apertures on the inner face.

Above and below: In 1948 a group of three La-11s took part in an expedition towards the North Pole which involved landing on an icefield. The purpose of the expedition was to check the possibility of using icefields as tactical airfields for the defence of the Soviet Polar regions.

Above and below: This La-11 was preserved in the Soviet Air Force Museum in Monino. It is seen here hangared in company with (left to right) a Tupolev Tu-2 bomber, a Yakovlev Yak-11 primary trainer, a Lisunov Li-2T transport and a Yak-12A liaison aircraft. Note the red star on the spinner.

following year it was transferred to an airfield at Dal'niy (Talien).

Not infrequently the La-11s deployed in China had tussles with USAF Lockheed P-38 Lightnings and North American P-51D Mustangs. One of these encounters took place on 2nd April 1951, and it ended in a dismal setback for the US pilots. On that morning a pair of La-11s led by the Soviet pilot Goozhov intercepted and destroyed two Mustangs which had intruded into Chinese airspace.

On 13 June 1951 the regiment was redeployed to Anshan near the North Korean border; two weeks later it joined the action, repelling the US air raids against the cities and industrial facilities of North Korea. Since the Soviet Union was not formally involved in the war, the fighters wore North Korean insignia for appearance's sake, though the La-11 was also flown by real North Koreans fighting in the Joint Chinese/Korean Air Army.

The La-11's first 'kill' in the Korean War was scored by Lieutenant V. Koorganov, a pilot of the 2nd Squadron, in the autumn of 1951; he shot down a Douglas B-26 Invader (the type was the USAF's main night bomber in Korea). Tackling this veteran of the Second World War in combat presented no difficulty. Intercepting the B-29, however, was a much more arduous task. Usually the Superfortresses flew their missions at about 10,000 m (32,800 ft); it took the La-11s no less than 26 minutes to reach that altitude. At its service ceiling the La-11 possessed only a marginal speed advantage over the B-29, not more than 20 km/h (12.4 mph), so the fighter's chances to score a victory were slender. All the more so, since the US pilots entered a shallow glide and easily made off towards the sea, once they were aware of the chase. Besides, the muzzle flash of the cannon dazzled the fighter pilot during night attacks. Not a single victory over the B-29 in the Korean War was ever scored by La-11 pilots.

In early 1952 the 351st Fighter Regiment had only two squadrons – one equipped with MiG-15s and the other with La-11s. The remaining 12 piston-engined fighters continued to fly combat missions as a part of the regiment until the summer of the following year; as before, their main adversary was the B-26.

Top left and centre left: This La-11 coded '83 White' somersaulted during a messed-up landing. Judging by the extent of the damage, the fighter was declared a total loss.

Above left: 351st IAP La-11s in Chinese markings in Shanghai; the red/white striped rudders were part of the PLAAF insignia until 1950. The second aircraft from the camera is coded '26 Yellow'.

Left: An instructor explains dogfight tactics to a group of North Korean pilots, with a North Korean La-11 coded '23 Red' as a backdrop.

Specifications of Lavochkin piston-engined fighters

	I-301	LaGG-3 production	LaGG-3 production	LaGG-3 production	LaGG-3-37	LaGG-3	'105' No.1	'105' No.2	LaGG-3M-82	La-5 production	La-5F production	La-5	La-5 dooblyor	La-5FN production	La-5UTI	La-5M-71	La-5TK
Year of production	1940	1941	1941	1942	1942	1942	1943	1943	1942	1942	1943	1943	1943	1943	1943	1943	1943
Powerplant	M-105P	M-105P	M-105P	M-105PA	M-105PF	M-105PF	M-105PF	M-105PF-2	M-82	M-82	M-82F	M-82	M-82FN	ASh-82FN	M-82	M-71	ASh-82FNV
Power at altitude: hp	1,050	1,050	1,050	1,050	1,180	1,180	1,180	1,240	1,330	1,330	1,330	1,330	1,470	1,470	1,330	1,870	1,470
kW	783	783	783	783	880	880	880	925	992	992	992	992	1,096	1,096	992	1,245	1,096
Length overall	8.81 m (28' 11")	8.81 m (28' 11")	8.82 m (28' 11")	8.82 m (28' 11")	8.9 m (29' 2¼")	8.82 m (28' 11")	8.82 m (28' 11")	8.82 m (28' 11")	8.71 m (28' 6¾")	8.7 m (28' 6½")	8.67 m (28' 5¼")	8.67 m (28' 5¼")	8.67 m (28' 5¼")	8.67 m (28' 5¼")	8.71 m (28' 6¾")	n.a.	8.67 m (28' 5¼")
Wingspan	9.8 m (32' 1¾")	9.8 m (32' 1¾")	9.8 m (32' 1¾")	9.8 m (32' 1¾")	9.8 m (32' 1¾")	9.8 m (32' 1¾")	9.8 m (32' 1¾")	9.8 m (32' 1¾")	9.8 m (32' 1¾")	9.6 m (31' 6")	9.6 m (31' 6")	9.6 m (31' 6")	9.8 m (32' 1¾")	9.8 m (32' 1¾")	9.6 m (31' 6")	n.a.	9.8 m (32' 1¾")
Wing area, m² (ft²)	17.51 (188.4)	17.51 (188.4)	17.51 (188.4)	17.51 (188.4)	17.51 (188.4)	17.51 (188.4)	17.51 (188.4)	17.51 (188.4)	17.51 (188.4)	17.37 (186.9)	17.27 (185.8)	17.27 (185.8)	17.27 (185.8)	17.59 (189.3)	17.37 (186.9)	17.56 (189.0)	17.56 (189.0)
Empty weight, kg (lb)	2,478 (5,482)	2,573 (5,672)	2,610 (5,753)	2,531 (5,579)	2,832 (6,243)	n.a.	2,234 (4,925)	2,285 (5,037)	2,790 (6,150)	2,681 (5,910)	2,590 (5,709)	2,600 (5,731)	2,582 (5,692)	2,678 (5,903)	2,576 (5,679)	2,840 (6,261)	n.a.
Gross weight, kg (lb)	2,968 (6,543)	3,346 (7,376)	3,280 (7,231)	3,100 (6,834)	3,363 (7,414)	2,865 (6,316)	2,818 (6,212)	2,875 (6,338)	3,380 (7,451)	3,360 (7,407)	3,220 (7,098)	3,200 (7,054)	3,166 (6,984)	3,322 (7,323)	3,210 (7,076)	3,526 (7,773)	n.a.
Top speed at sea level, km/h (mph)	515.0 (320.0)	498.0 (309.4)	457.0 (283.9)	446.0 (277.1)	501.0 (311.3)	497.0 (308.8)	541.0 (336.1)	554.0 (344.2)	515.0 (320.0)	509.0 (316.2)	551.0 (342.3)	518.0 (321.8)	595.0 (369.7)	573.0 (356.0)	552.0 (343.0)	612.0 (380.2)	n.a.
Top speed at altitude, km/h (mph)	605.0 (375.9)	575.0 (357.2)	535.0 (332.4)	518.0 (332.4)	560.0 (347.9)	564.0 (350.4)	612.0 (380.2)	618.0 (384.0)	600.0 (372.8)	580.0 (360.4)	590.0 (366.6)	600.0 (372.8)	648.0 (402.6)	620.0 (385.2)	600.0 (372.8)	685.0 (425.6)	n.a.
@ m (ft)	4,950 (16,250)	5,000 (16,400)	5,000 (16,400)	5,100 (16,750)	4,100 (13,500)	4,000 (13,000)	3,400 (11,250)	3,400 (11,250)	6,450 (21,000)	6,250 (20,500)	6,150 (20,000)	6,500 (21,250)	6,300 (20,750)	6,150 (20,000)	2,300 (7,500)	5,500 (18,000)	n.a.
Climb to 5,000 m (16,400 ft), min	5.85	6.8	8.5	7.1	7.3	6.0	5.1	4.8	6.0	6.0	5.5	6.1	4.7	4.7	5.7	n.a.	n.a.
Service ceiling, m (ft)	9,600 (31,500)	9,100 (29,750)	9,300 (30,500)	9,300 (30,500)	9,000 (29,500)	10,200 (33,500)	10,250 (33,750)	10,750 (35,250)	n.a.	9,500 (31,000)	9,550 (31,250)	9,650 (31,750)	11,200 (36,750)	10,700 (35,000)	n.a.	n.a.	n.a.
Turn time, seconds	20	n.a.	20	26	22	19	n.a.	n.a.	25	22.6	20	19	18.5	19	19	n.a.	n.a.
Operational range, km (miles)	556 (345)	870 (540)	705 (438)	466 (289)	n.a.	n.a.	n.a.	535 (332)	n.a.	655 (407)	450 (279)	900 (559)	480 (298)	580 (360)	n.a.	n.a.	n.a.
Take-off run, m (ft)	355 (1,164)	500 (1,640)	545 (1,788)	515 (1,689)	465 (1,525)	n.a.	188 (616)	n.a.	310 (1,017)	400 (1,312)	350 (1,148)	n.a.	285 (935)	290 (951)	350 (1,148)	n.a.	n.a.
Landing roll, m (ft)	400 (1,312)	460 (1,509)	460 (1,509)	560 (1,837)	610 (2,001)	n.a.	n.a.	n.a.	470 (1,541)	500 (1,640)	475 (1,558)	n.a.	485 (1,591)	510 (1,673)	475 (1,558)	n.a.	n.a.
Armament (mm)	1x23 2x12.7	3x12.7 2x7.62	1x20 1x12.7	1x20 1x12.7	1x37 1x12.7	1x20 1x12.7	1x20 1x12.7	1x23 1x12.7	2x20	2x20	2x20	1x20 1x12.7	2x20	2x20	1x20	2x20	2x20

Specifications of Lavochkin piston-engined fighters (continued)

	La-5 c/n 39210206	La-5*	La-7 production	La-7 production	La-7TK	La-7ASh-71	La-7UTI	'120'	'126'	'130'	La-9 ('130')	'132'	'132M'	La-9UTI ('140')	La-9M ('134D')	La-11
Year of Production	1943	1944	1944	1945	1944	1944	1945	1945	1945	1946	1946	1946	1946**	1947	1947	1947
Powerplant	M-82FN	ASh-82FN	ASh-82FN	ASh-82FN	ASh-82FN	ASh-71	ASh-82FN	ASh-83	n.a.	M-83	ASh-82FN	M-93	M-82M	ASh-82FN	ASh-82FN	ASh-82FN
Power at altitude: hp	1,470	1,470	1,470	1,470	1,470	2,000	1,470	1,900	n.a.	1,900	1,470	n.a.	n.a.	1,470	1,470	1,470
kW	1,096	1,096	1,096	1,096	1,096	1,492	1,096	1,416		1,416	1,096			1,096	1,096	1,096
Length overall	n.a.	8.6 m (28' 2½")	8.6 m (28' 2½")	8.6 m (28' 2½")	8.6 m (28' 2½")	n.a.	n.a.	8.642 m (28' 4¼")	n.a.	n.a.	8.625 m (28' 3½")	8.625 m (28' 3½")	n.a.	n.a.	8.62 m (28' 3⅜")	8.62 m (28' 3⅜")
Wingspan	9.8 m (32' 1¾")	9.8 m (32' 1¾")	9.8 m (32' 1¾")	9.8 m (32' 1¾")	9.8 m (32' 1¾")	9.8 m (32' 1¾")	9.8 m (32' 1¾")	9.8 m (32' 1¾")	n.a.	n.a.	9.8 m (32' 1¾")	9.8 m (32' 1¾")	n.a.	9.8 m (32' 1¾")	10.28 m (33' 8¾")	9.8 m (32' 1¾")
Wing area, m^2 (ft^2)	17.59 (189.3)	17.59 (189.3)	17.59 (189.3)	17.59 (189.3)	17.59 (189.3)	17.59 (189.3)	17.59 (189.3)	n.a.	n.a.	n.a.	17.59 (189.3)	n.a.	n.a.	17.59 (189.3)	17.59 (189.3)	17.59 (189.3)
Empty weight, kg (lb)	n.a.	2,605 (5,742)	n.a.	n.a.	2,711 (5,976)	2,849 (6,280)	2,724 (6,005)	n.a.	n.a.	n.a.	2,638 (5,815)	n.a.	n.a.	2,554 (5,630)	2,934 (6,468)	2,770 (6,105)
Gross weight, kg (lb)	3,445 (7,594)	3,265 (7,197)	3,250 7,184)	3,315 (7,308)	3,280 (7,231)	3,505 (7,727)	3,372 (7,433)	3,140 (6,920)	3,287 (7,246)	3,560 (7,850)	3,425 (7,550)	3,580 (7,890)	n.a.	3,285 (7,242)	n.a.	3,730 (8,220)
Top speed at sea level, km/h (mph)	630.0 (391.4)	597.0 (370.9)	612.0 (380.2)	613.0 (380.9)	600.0 (372.8)	n.a.	n.a.	604.0 (375,1)	630.0 (391,3)	630.0 (391,3)	640.0 (397.5)	650.0 (403.7)	630.0 (391,3)	558.0 (346.5)	590.0 (366.4)	562.0 (349.0)
Top speed at altitude, km/h (mph)	684.0 (425.0)	680.0 (422.5)	658.0 (408.8)	661,0 (410.7)	676.0 (420.0)	n.a.	n.a.	725.0 (451.3)	690.0 (428.5)	725.0 (451.3)	690.0 (428.5)	740.0 (459.6)	730.0 (453.4)	659.0 (409.3)	675.0 (419.2)	562.0 (349.0)
@ m (ft)	6,150 (20,000)	6,000 (19,750)	5,900 (19,250)	6,000 (19,750)	8,000 (26,250)	n.a.	n.a.	7,400 (24,280)	6,000 (19,685)	7,500 (24,600)	6,250 (20,500)	6,500 (21,320)	5,000 (16,400)	6,200 (20,340)	6,100 (20,010)	6,200 (20,340)
Climb to 5,000 m (16,400ft), min	5.2	4.45	5.1	5.3	4.5	n.a.	n.a.	4.9	4.6	5.0	4.7	4.8	4.8	5.0	6.4	6.6
Service ceiling, m (ft)	n.a.	10,750 (35,250)	11,300 (37,000)	10,450 (34,250)	11,800 (38,750)	n.a.	n.a.	11,600 (38,060)	11,000 (36,090)	10,500 (34,450)	10,800 (35,430)	12,000 (39.370)	11,500 (37,730)	11,125 (36,500)	10,000 (32,810)	10,250 (33,630)
Turn time, seconds	n.a.	n.a.	20.5	n.a.	n.a.	n.a.	n.a.	n.a.	n.a.	n.a.	20-21	n.a.	n.a.	n.a.	n.a.	24-25
Operational range, km (miles)	n.a.	n.a.	665 (413)	n.a.	n.a.	n.a.	n.a.	n.a.	900 (559)	1,450 (900)	1,950 (1,210)	1,200 (745)	1,000 (621)	955 (593)	3,250 (2,020)	2,535 (1,575)
Take-off run, m (ft)	n.a.	n.a.	340 (1,115)	350 (1,148)	n.a.	n.a.	n.a.	n.a.	n.a.	n.a.	345 (1,130)	n.a.	300 (985)	370 (1,210)	450 (1,480)	535 (1,755)
Landing roll , m (ft)	n.a.	n.a.	540 (1,771)	n.a.	n.a.	n.a.	n.a.	n.a.	n.a.	n.a.	490 (1,610)	n.a.	400 (1,310)	410 (1,345)	n.a.	600 (1,970)
Armament (mm)	2x20 1x12.7	3x20 1x12	2x20	3x20	2x20	2x20	1x20	2x23	4x23	4x23	4x23	4x23	4x23	1x23	3x23	3x23

***** Etalon (standard-setter) for 1944

** Project only

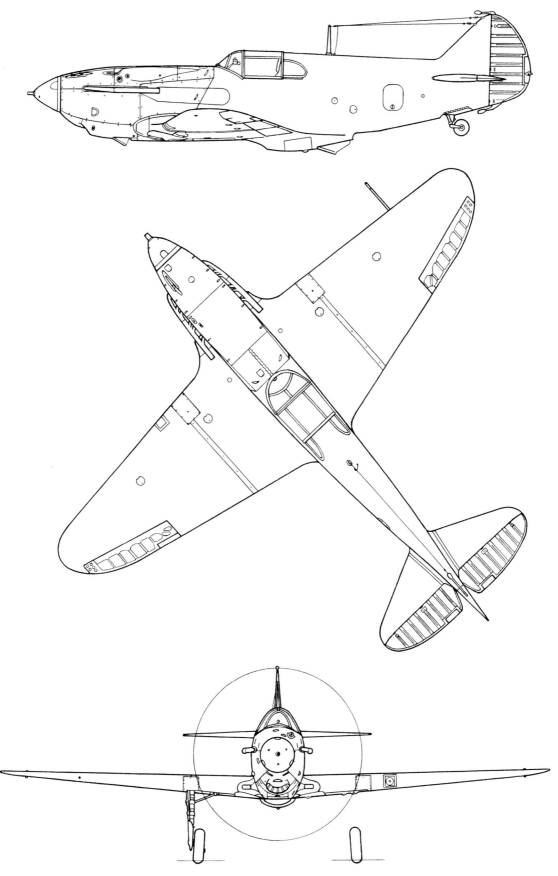

An early-production Gor'kiy-built or Taganrog-built LaGG-3.

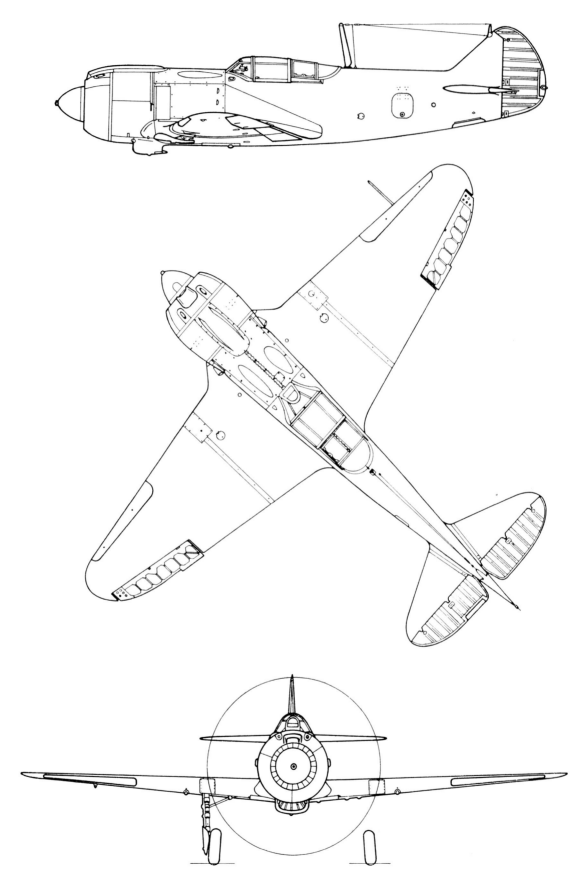

A typical production La-5FN.

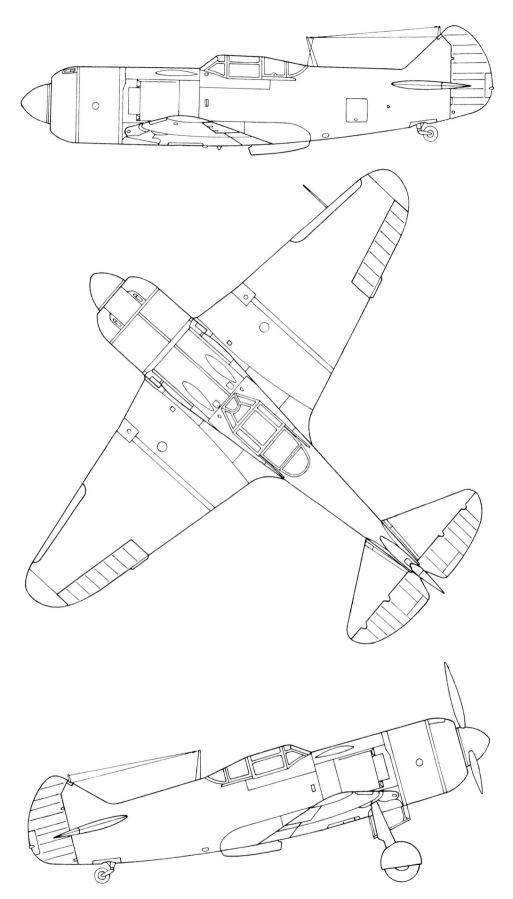

A typical production La-7.

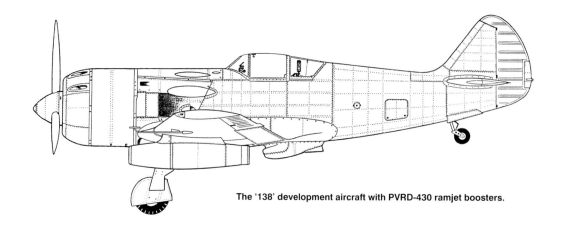

The '138' development aircraft with PVRD-430 ramjet boosters.

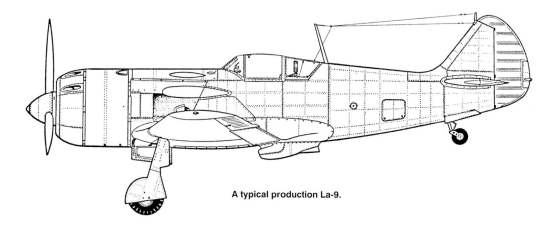

A typical production La-9.

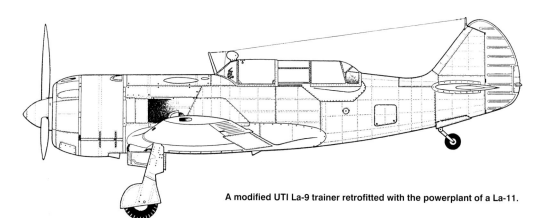

A modified UTI La-9 trainer retrofitted with the powerplant of a La-11.

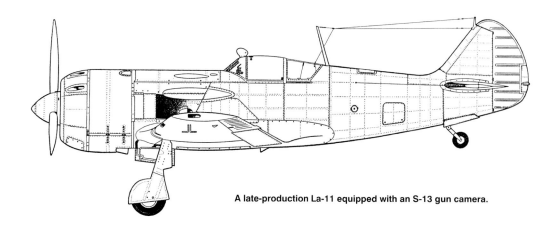

A late-production La-11 equipped with an S-13 gun camera.

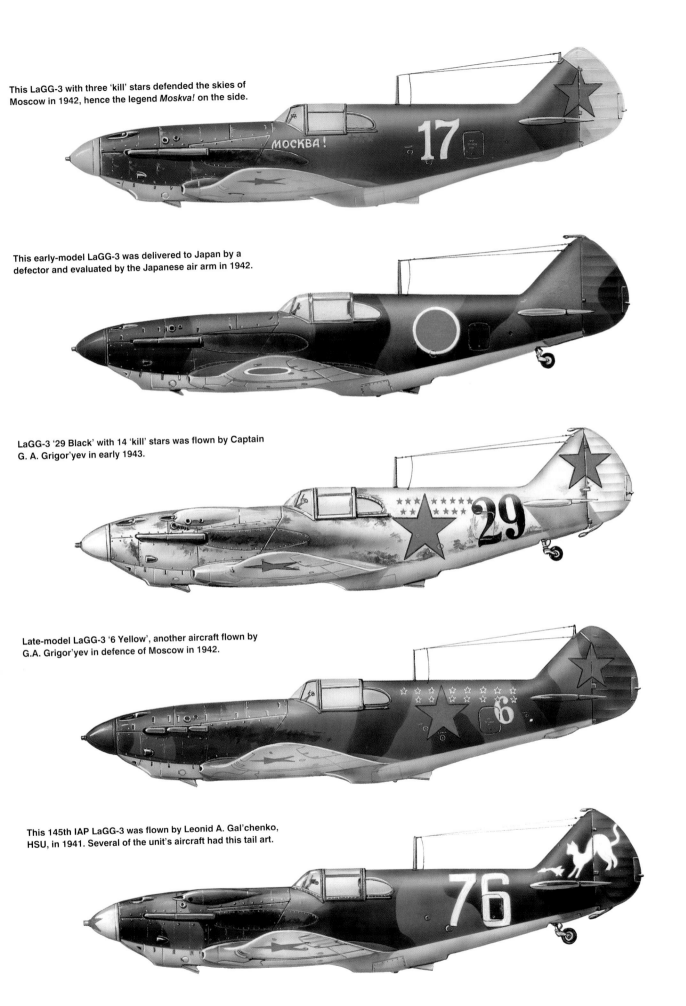

This LaGG-3 with three 'kill' stars defended the skies of Moscow in 1942, hence the legend *Moskva!* on the side.

This early-model LaGG-3 was delivered to Japan by a defector and evaluated by the Japanese air arm in 1942.

LaGG-3 '29 Black' with 14 'kill' stars was flown by Captain G. A. Grigor'yev in early 1943.

Late-model LaGG-3 '6 Yellow', another aircraft flown by G.A. Grigor'yev in defence of Moscow in 1942.

This 145th IAP LaGG-3 was flown by Leonid A. Gal'chenko, HSU, in 1941. Several of the unit's aircraft had this tail art.

This Batch 66 Tbilisi-built LaGG-3 was flown by Yuriy Schchipov, Black Sea Fleet Air Arm, in 1944.

This late-production LaGG-3 still retains traces of temporary winter camouflage.

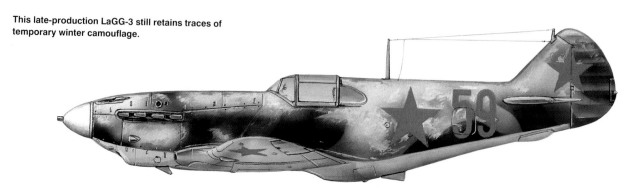

'30 Red', a well-weathered LaGG-3 of the Red Banner Baltic Fleet Air Arm flown by S. I. L'vov in the winter of 1943.

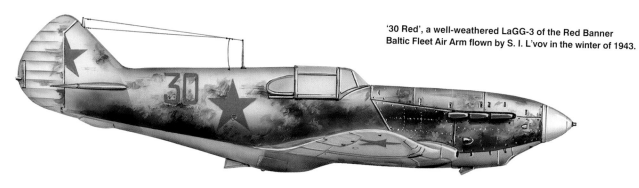

LG-3, one of three captured LaGG-3s to be made airworthy and operated by the Finnish Air Force.

La-5 '24 White' saw action on the Leningrad Front in 1943.

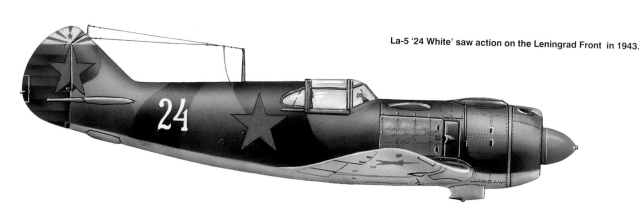

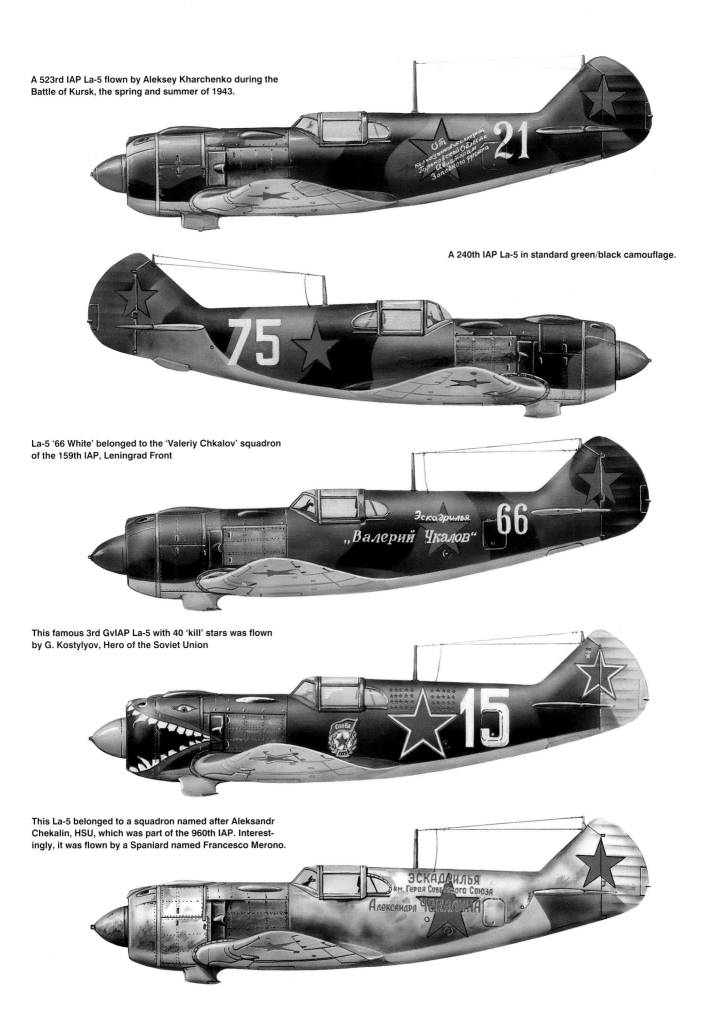

A 523rd IAP La-5 flown by Aleksey Kharchenko during the Battle of Kursk, the spring and summer of 1943.

A 240th IAP La-5 in standard green/black camouflage.

La-5 '66 White' belonged to the 'Valeriy Chkalov' squadron of the 159th IAP, Leningrad Front

This famous 3rd GvIAP La-5 with 40 'kill' stars was flown by G. Kostylyov, Hero of the Soviet Union

This La-5 belonged to a squadron named after Aleksandr Chekalin, HSU, which was part of the 960th IAP. Interestingly, it was flown by a Spaniard named Francesco Merono.

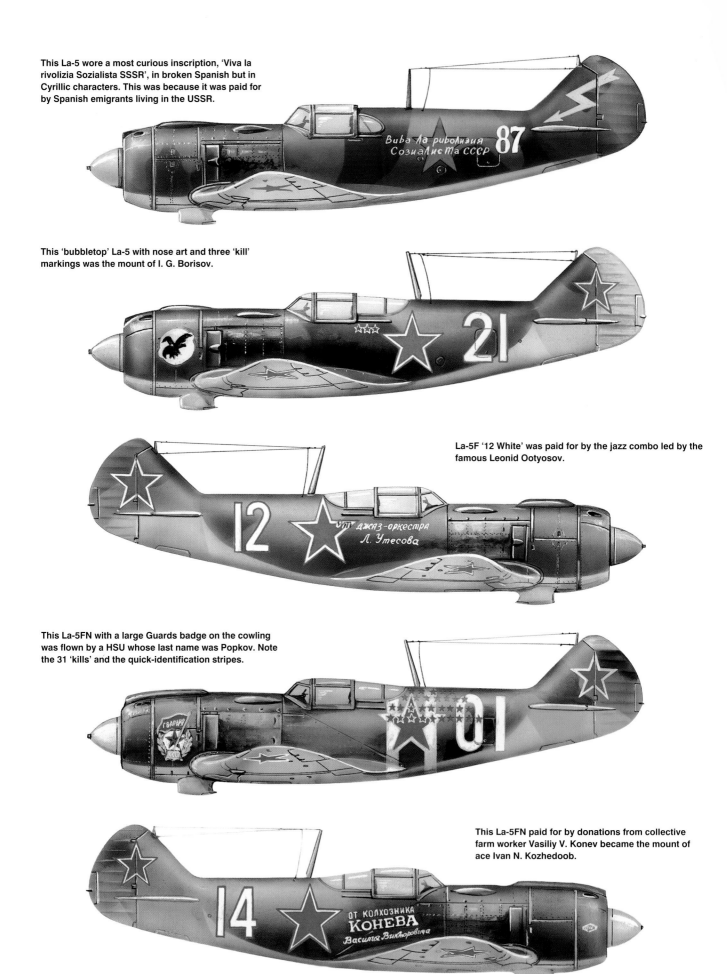

This La-5 wore a most curious inscription, 'Viva la rivolizia Sozialista SSSR', in broken Spanish but in Cyrillic characters. This was because it was paid for by Spanish emigrants living in the USSR.

This 'bubbletop' La-5 with nose art and three 'kill' markings was the mount of I. G. Borisov.

La-5F '12 White' was paid for by the jazz combo led by the famous Leonid Ootyosov.

This La-5FN with a large Guards badge on the cowling was flown by a HSU whose last name was Popkov. Note the 31 'kills' and the quick-identification stripes.

This La-5FN paid for by donations from collective farm worker Vasiliy V. Konev became the mount of ace Ivan N. Kozhedoob.

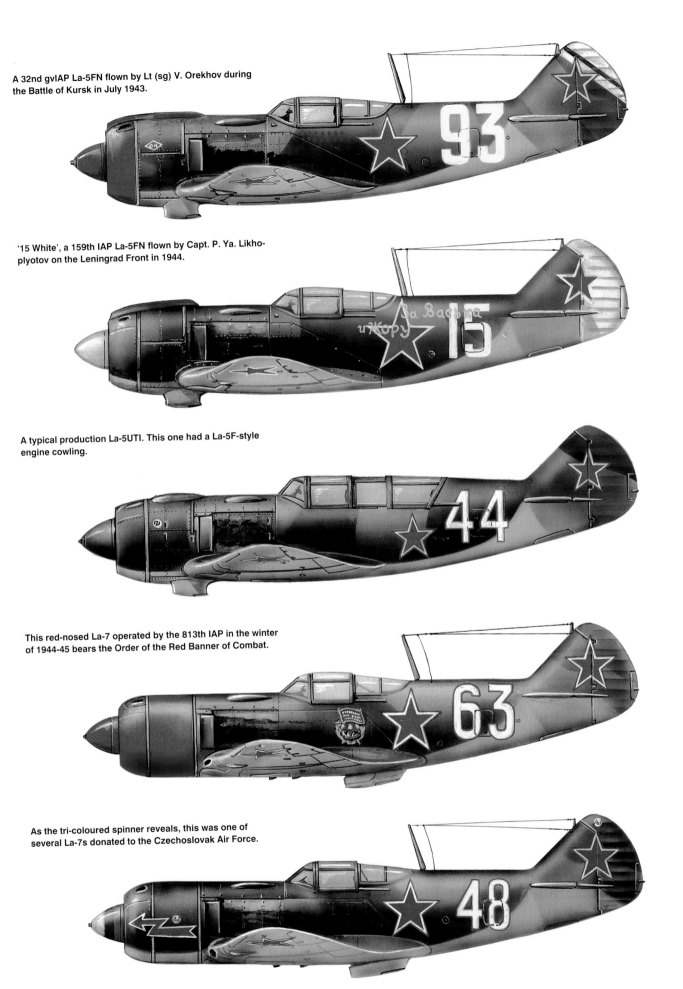

A 32nd gvIAP La-5FN flown by Lt (sg) V. Orekhov during the Battle of Kursk in July 1943.

'15 White', a 159th IAP La-5FN flown by Capt. P. Ya. Likho-plyotov on the Leningrad Front in 1944.

A typical production La-5UTI. This one had a La-5F-style engine cowling.

This red-nosed La-7 operated by the 813th IAP in the winter of 1944-45 bears the Order of the Red Banner of Combat.

As the tri-coloured spinner reveals, this was one of several La-7s donated to the Czechoslovak Air Force.

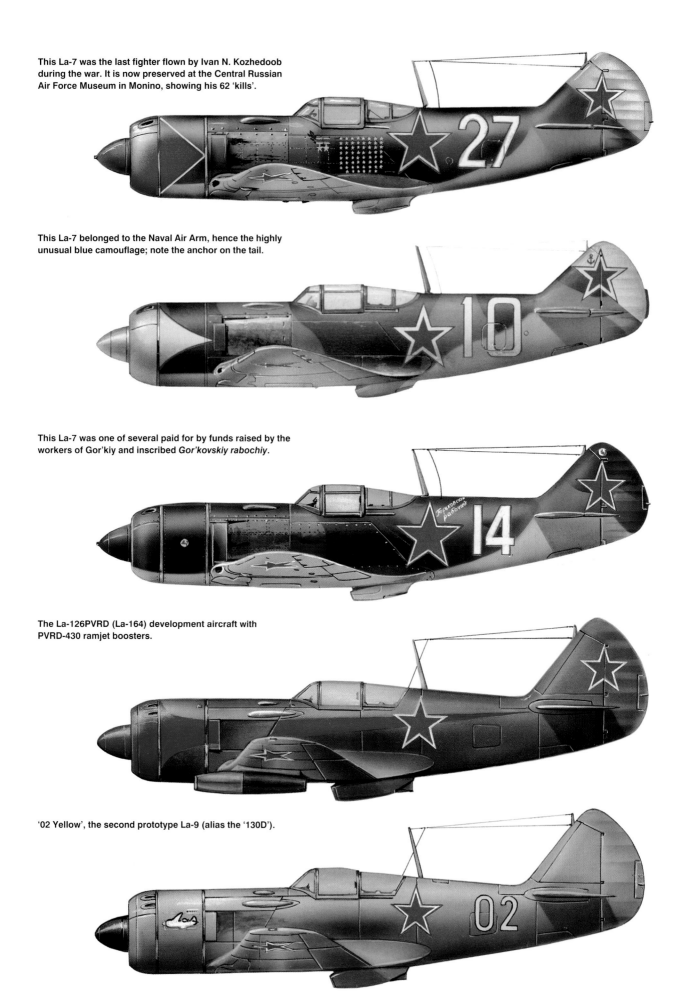

This La-7 was the last fighter flown by Ivan N. Kozhedoob during the war. It is now preserved at the Central Russian Air Force Museum in Monino, showing his 62 'kills'.

This La-7 belonged to the Naval Air Arm, hence the highly unusual blue camouflage; note the anchor on the tail.

This La-7 was one of several paid for by funds raised by the workers of Gor'kiy and inscribed *Gor'kovskiy rabochiy*.

The La-126PVRD (La-164) development aircraft with PVRD-430 ramjet boosters.

'02 Yellow', the second prototype La-9 (alias the '130D').

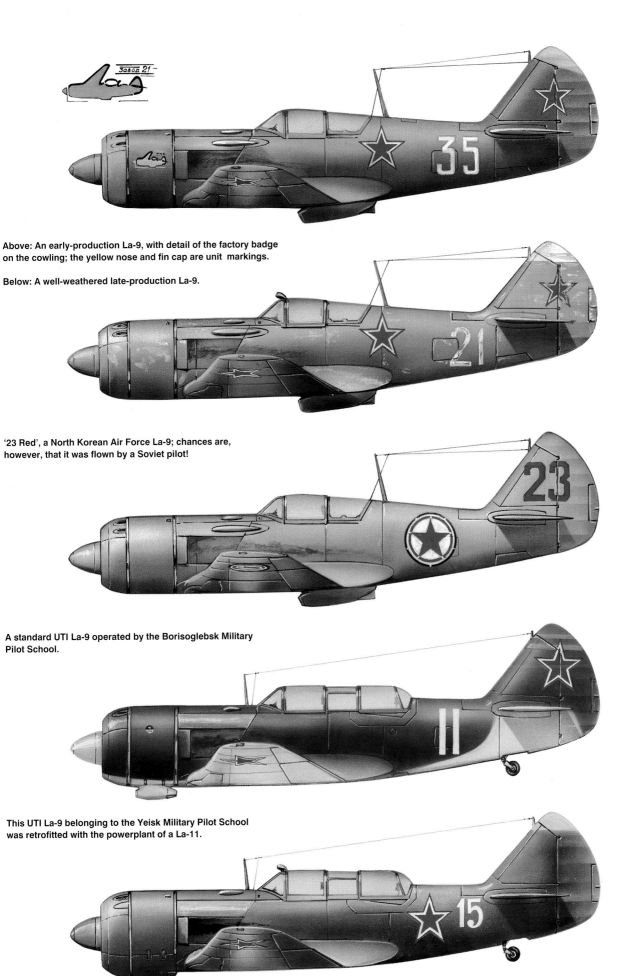

Above: An early-production La-9, with detail of the factory badge on the cowling; the yellow nose and fin cap are unit markings.

Below: A well-weathered late-production La-9.

'23 Red', a North Korean Air Force La-9; chances are, however, that it was flown by a Soviet pilot!

A standard UTI La-9 operated by the Borisoglebsk Military Pilot School.

This UTI La-9 belonging to the Yeisk Military Pilot School was retrofitted with the powerplant of a La-11.

This UTI La-9 in Chinese markings was operated by a
Soviet unit, the 351st IAP based in Shanghai.

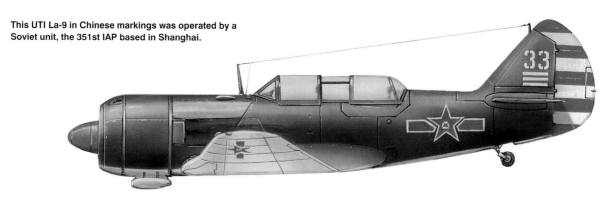

The prototype of the La-9 with RD-13 pulse-jet boosters.

The '132' development aircraft.

The first prototype of the '134' development aircraft

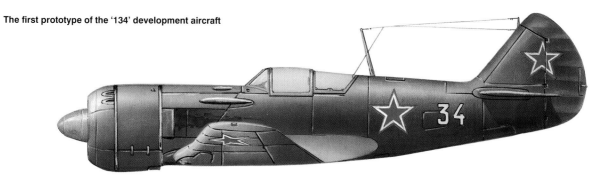

The uncoded '134D' second prototype with tip tanks in place.

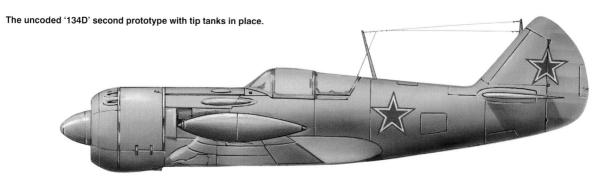

Ла-11

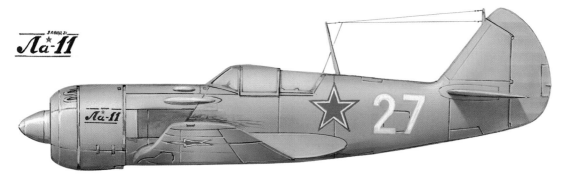

Above: This La-11 was one of several which accompanied a pair of Tu-4 bombers on a flight over the North Pole in April 1950.

Below: This La-11 in a highly unusual cherry-red finish was delivered to the 911th IAP in Ust'-Kut.

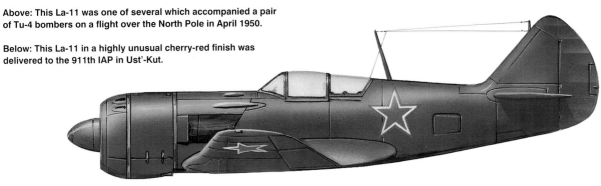

This La-9 in Chinese markings was in fact operated by the 351st IAP and based in Shanghai.

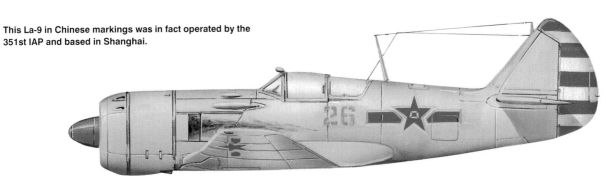

La-11 '02 Yellow' was flown by N. I. Goozhov, a 351st IAP pilot, in 1950. The tail stripes were deleted that year.

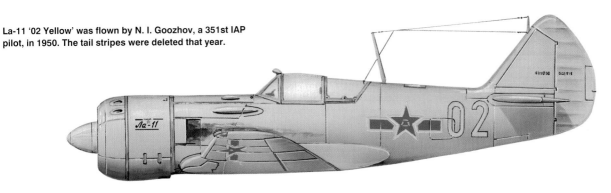

Korean La-11s received various camouflage patterns towards the end of the Korean War (1953).

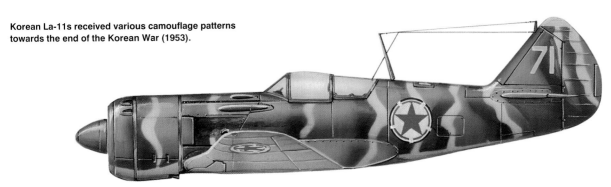

Above: La-7 '77 White' in the Military Museum (VM VHÚ) at Prague-Kbely. This aircraft was once operated by the Czechoslovak Air Force in this guise, later gaining CzAF markings; the original colour scheme was restored after preservation.

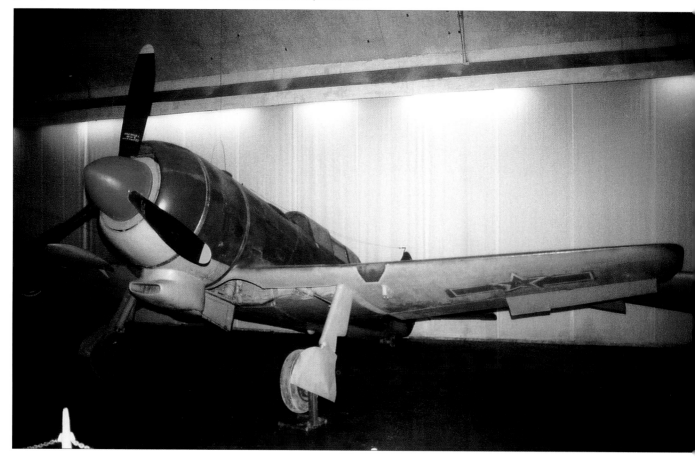

A Chinese People's Liberation Army Air Force UTI La-9 in the PLAAF Museum at Datang Shan AB near Beijing.

Above: La-9 '06 Red' preserved at Datang Shan wears the PLAAF 'stars and bars' insignia (the use of red and white rudder stripes was discontinued after 1950), though the darker spot on the aft fuselage suggests it may have worn North Korean markings at an earlier date.

Another view of the La-11 in the PLAAF Museum. The hangars at Datang Shan generally offer rather challenging conditions for the photographer!

Above: One more view of La-9 '06 Red'. Like their sister aircraft in Soviet service, the Chinese La-9s usually wore a light grey air superiority colour scheme.

This green-painted La-9 preserved in the Armed Forces Museum in Beijing is not so lucky, being displayed in the open – with a resulting deterioration in its condition.

bove: La-11 '24 Red' preserved at Datang Shan wears North Korean markings.

he Armed Forces Museum im Beijing also boasts a La-11 – again in less-than-perfect condition.

Red Star Volume 3
POLIKARPOV'S I-16 FIGHTER

Yefim Gordon and Keith Dexter

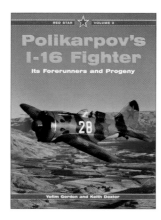

Often dismissed because it did not fare well against its more modern adversaries in the Second World War, Nikolay Polikarpov's I-16 was nevertheless an outstanding fighter – among other things, because it was the world's first monoplane fighter with a retractable undercarriage. Its capabilities were demonstrated effectively during the Spanish Civil War. Covers every variant, from development, unbuilt projects and the later designs that evolved from it.

Sbk, 280 x 215 mm, 128 pages, 185 b/w photographs, 17 pages of colour artworks, plus line drawings
1 85780 131 8 **£18.99/US $27.95**

Red Star Volume 4
EARLY SOVIET JET FIGHTERS

Yefim Gordon

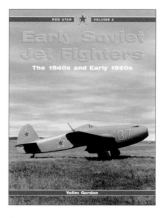

This charts the development and service history of the first-generation Soviet jet fighters designed by such renowned 'fighter makers' as Mikoyan, Yakovlev and Sukhoi, as well as design bureaux no longer in existence – the Lavochkin and Alekseyev OKBs, during the 1940s and early 1950s. Each type is detailed and compared to other contemporary jet fighters. As ever the extensive photo coverage includes much which is previously unseen.

Sbk, 280 x 215 mm, 144 pages 240 b/w and 9 colour photos, 8 pages of colour artworks
1 85780 139 3 **£19.99/US $29.95**

Red Star Volume 5
YAKOVLEV'S PISTON-ENGINED FIGHTERS

Yefim Gordon & Dmitriy Khazanov

This authoritative monograph describ this entire family from the simple but rugged and agile Yak-1 through the Yak-7 (born as a trainer but eventually developed into a fighter) and the proli and versatile Yak-9 to the most capab of the line, the Yak-3 with which even the aces of the Luftwaffe were relucta to tangle. Yak piston fighters also served outside Russia and several examples can be seen in flying condition in the west.

Sbk, 280 x 215 mm, 144 pages, 313 b/w and 2 col photos, 7pp of colour artworks, 8pp of line drawings
1 85780 140 7 **£19.99/US $29.95**

Red Star Volume 6
POLIKARPOV'S BIPLANE FIGHTERS

Yefim Gordon and Keith Dexter

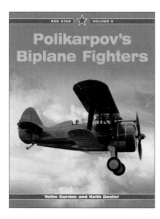

The development of Polikarpov's fighting biplanes including the 2I-N1, the I-3, and I-5, which paved the way for the I-15 which earned fame as the Chato during the Spanish Civil War and saw action against the Japanese; the I-15*bis* and the famous I-153 Chaika retractable gear gull-wing biplane. Details of combat use are given, plus structural descriptions, details of the ill-starred I-190, and of privately owned I-15*bis* and I-153s restored to fly.

Softback, 280 x 215 mm, 128 pages c250 b/w and colour photos; three-view drawings, 60+ colour side views
1 85780 141 5 **£18.99/US $27.95**

Red Star Volume 7
TUPOLEV Tu-4 SOVIET SUPERFORTRESS

Yefim Gordon and Vladimir Rigmant

At the end of WW2, three Boeing B-29s fell into Soviet hands; from these came a Soviet copy of this famous bomber in the form of the Tu-4. This examines the evolution of the 'Superfortresski' and its further development into the Tu-70 transport. It also covers the civil airliner version, the Tu-75, and the Tu-85, the last of Tupolev's piston-engined bombers. Also described are various experimental versions, including the Burlaki towed fighter programme.

Sbk, 280 x 215 mm, 128pp, 225 b/w and 9 colour photos, plus line drawings
1 85780 142 3 **£18.99/US $27.95**

Red Star Volume 8
RUSSIA'S EKRANOPLANS
Caspian Sea Monster and other WIG Craft

Sergey Komissarov

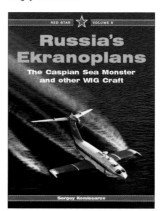

Known as wing-in-ground effect (WIGE) craft or by their Russian name of ekranoplan, these vehicles operate on the borderline between the sky and sea, offering the speed of an aircraft coupled with better operating economics and the ability to operate pretty much anywhere on the world's waterways.

WIGE vehicles by various design bureaus are covered, including the Orlyonok, the only ekranoplan to see squadron service, the Loon and the KM, or Caspian Sea Monster.

Sbk, 280 x 215 mm, 128 pages 150 b/w and colour photos, plus dwgs
1 85780 146 6 **£18.99/US $27.95**

Red Star Volume 9
TUPOLEV Tu-160 BLACKJAC
Russia's Answer to the B-1

Yefim Gordon

How the Soviet Union's most poten strategic bomber was designed, bu and put into service. Comparison is made between the Tu-160 and the Sukhoi T-4 ('aircraft 100', a bombe which was ahead of its time), the variable-geometry 'aircraft 200' – and the Myasishchev M-18 and M-2

Included are copies of original factory drawings of the Tu-160, M-1 M-20 and several other intriguing projects. Richly illustrated in colour many shots taken at Engels.

Sbk, 280 x 215 mm, 128pp, 193 col b/w photos, dwgs, colour side views
1 85780 147 4 **£18.99/US $27.95**